WHEN THE CHURCH BELL RANG RACIST

WHEN THE CHURCH BELL RANG RACIST

THE METHODIST CHURCH AND THE CIVIL RIGHTS MOVEMENT IN ALABAMA

Donald E. Collins

Mercer University Press
Macon, Georgia

ISBN 0-86554-605-3   MUP/H456

Copyright ©1998
Mercer University Press, Macon, Georgia 31210-3960 USA
All rights reserved
Printed in the United States of America

The paper used in this publication meets the minimum require-
ments of American National Standard for Information Sciences—Per-
manence of Paper for Printed Library Materials, ANSI Z39.48-1984.

Library of Congress Cataloging-in-Publication Data

Collins, Donald E.,
    When the Church Bell Rang Racist: The Methodist Church and
    the Civil Rights Movement in Alabama / Donald E. Collins
        xii + 178 pp.   6" x 9" (15 x 22 cm.)
    Includes bibiliographical references and index.
    ISBN 0-86554-605-3 (alk. paper)
    1.   Afro-Americans—Civil   Rights—Alabama—History—20th
century. 2 Afro-Americans—Civil Rights—Florida—History—20th
century. 3. Methodist Church—Alabama—History—20th century. 4.
Methodist Church—Florida—History—20th century. 5. Civil rights
movements— Alabama—History—20th century. 6. Civil rights
movements—Florida—History—20th century. 7. Racism—Religious
aspects—Methodists—History—20th century. 8. Alabama—Race
relations. 9. Florida—Race relations.   I. Title
F335.N4C65 1998
323.1'1960761—dc21
                                                    98-45100
                                                    CIP

To those with whom I shared
a passion, dream, commitment, and
will to make a difference—
Charles, Dan, Andrew, Powers, James,
Welton, Tom, Joe Neal, J.B., Max, Stan,
and others.

CONTENTS

Preface ix

Introduction: The History, Organization,
    and Ministry of the Methodist Church 3

1. The Loss of Innocence: 1950-1955 9

2. Taking Sides: 1955-1956 23

3. Tuskegee and Mobile : 1957-1958 35

4. White Resistance Intensifies: 1958-1959 49

5. Methodist Layman's Union vs. the Sit-ins: 1960-1961 57

6. The Seeds of Hate Bear Fruit: 1962-1963 73

7. Alabama Catches Its Breath: 1964 89

8. Violence and Death Return to Alabama: 1965 103

9. Token Integration and the Methodist Church: 1965 115

10. When Will the Church Bell Ring? 1966-1967 127

11. Agonizing and Defining Decisions: 1968-1972 143

12. The Church Bell Rings: 1973-1997 153

Bibliography 169

Index 175

ILLUSTRATIONS

Alabama-West Florida Conference Boundaries 12
Annual Meeting Notice of Methodist Layman's Union 61
Letter from Robert F. Kennedy 93
Bishop W. Kenneth Goodson's Pastoral Letter 112
Petition of Methodist Layman's Union 113
Resolution for the Elimination of Racial Structure 138-139
Churches of the Central Jurisdiction by District 153

PREFACE

SINCE ABOUT 400 C.E. CHURCH BELLS HAVE SIGNALED THE WELCOME of the Christian church to all who would hear its gospel. By the 900s it was customary to place the bells in towers that were designed as part of church buildings. At certain times and in certain places, however, racism has led the church to limit its welcome to its own kind. Most of the Southern white church during the civil rights movement fell victim to such prejudice and its bells welcomed only those who supported the segregated status quo. This book tells the story of a time when the church bell rang racist.

On April 4, 1968 the Reverend Maxwell Hale and an interracial group of ten students from Purdue University arrived at my home, the Ferry Pass Methodist Church parsonage in Pensacola, Florida. Max had been a close friend and colleague for many years. It was spring break and Max, the director of the Wesley Foundation at Purdue University, was taking these college students on a pilgrimage, visiting the sites in Alabama and elsewhere where many of the civil rights struggles of recent years had occurred. They had visited Birmingham, Tuscaloosa, Montgomery, Tuskegee, Auburn, Selma, Mobile, and were at our home in Pensacola to rest.

While the students played a game of touch football in our backyard, Max and I discussed the profound events that had engaged both of us during the last decade and the innocence of the students who had been astounded and moved by their odyssey.

Suddenly, my wife interrupted with an emotional, devastating jolt. Our close friend Charles Prestwood had just called to say that the news was reporting that Martin Luther King Jr., had been shot in Memphis. We quickly got the students out of the public eye and into the house. A biracial group of youth in the yard of a white, middle-class neighborhood of Pensacola was risky enough, but with the news that King had been shot, prudence required caution.

With the students inside, we watched the television to see if there was any hope, only to be stunned with the word that King was dead. The man who had led his people and the nation in a non-violent revolution had been gunned down on a motel balcony in Memphis. An irrecoverable force for human justice was gone. The best hope

America had of healing the scars of the 1950s and 1960s and holding high the dream of freedom, justice, and equality was ended.

I sat silently while the television announcer covered the details of the horror, my mind racing with images of Montgomery, Birmingham, Selma, the Lincoln Memorial, and other places and events that had touched my life and engaged my energies. I thought of the times I had met with King and members of his staff.

My role in the historic issues and experiences of the civil rights struggles was exceedingly small. By accident of birth and choice of profession, I was a Methodist minister in Alabama where great and divisive issues were being engaged by ordinary men. From the beginning to the end of the conflict, I joined with others in the cause of justice for all.

This book is the story of those years. This story's perspective is that of the Methodist Church in Alabama and its ministers, the perspective from which I and the other ministers saw and experienced the agony and tragedy of the 1950s and 1960s. The historic events that occurred in Alabama provide the framework around which the story unfolds. These events are not covered here in detail, but are merely referenced as the context and backdrop of the challenge that confronted the Methodist Church and its ministers during those stormy years. From the 1955-1956 Montgomery bus boycott to the 1965 Selma march and beyond, this narrative interweaves those struggles for change with the forces of resistance.

This account is as fair and as accurate as the records of those years and the memories of the many men and women who shared their painful experiences make possible. I do not presume that other stories could not be told and should not be included. I simply share my experiences and those of over fifty other Methodist ministers whom I interviewed for this book.

I am indebted to many who have made substantial contributions to the research and preparation of this book. After being away for over a quarter of a century from the place, the people, and the events that comprise this historical story, the personal and public records shared by a large group of individuals have been invaluable.

To the Commission on Archives and History of the Alabama-West Florida Conference, the United Methodist Church, and to its archivist, Mary Ann Pickard, I am indebted. She provided and made available many records, including Journals of the Alabama-West Florida Conference, and Disciplines of the Methodist Church covering more than forty-five years.

I am especially indebted to the more than fifty-five Methodist ministers of the Alabama-West Florida Conference who are my former colleagues and who responded to my interview requests. These men not only shared the details of their experiences, but they also searched their personal files and shared scores and scores of records and documents essential to the accurate preparation of this book.

Two of my friends, Donald G. Brown and O. C. Brown, read the initial draft and made suggestions of ideas, information, and editorial advice that vastly improved and helped give shape to the manuscript. And finally, I wish to thank my wife Betty and my son Jeffrey for their laborious contribution in reading and re-reading the manuscript as it developed. Every writer needs one or more persons who can objectively evaluate, critically question, and candidly convey to the writer needed changes and ideas. Betty and Jeffrey skillfully filled this role.

Rise up, O men of God!
His kingdom tarries long;
Bring in the day of brotherhood
And end the night of wrong.

—William P. Merrill

WHEN THE CHURCH BELL RANG RACIST

INTRODUCTION:

THE HISTORY, ORGANIZATION, AND MINISTRY OF THE METHODIST CHURCH

WHEN THE CHRISTMAS CONFERENCE MET IN 1784 IT WAS DIFFICULT to find a Methodist, but in 1810 there was one Methodist for every thirty-nine persons in America. In 1840, one out of every nineteen in the nation was Methodist . . . and by 1860 one third of American Protestants were Methodist.

—John O. Gross[1]

Central to an understanding of the impact of the civil rights movement on the Methodist Church, its ministers, members, and programs in Alabama is the need to discern, at least in cursory fashion, the history, organization, and ministry of the Methodist Church. Without such a review of the institution, understanding and following the actions, interworking relationships, and behavior of the Methodist Church would be impossible. This kind of understanding must begin with a synoptic history of American Methodism and its many divisive splits and reunifications.

METHODIST HISTORY

American Methodism was formally organized as a denomination at a Christmas conference in 1784 in Baltimore, Maryland. Formed from what had been called Methodist Societies, the new church called itself the Methodist Episcopal Church. Between 1784 and 1870 this new American church grew and expanded as the nation grew, but during those years it experienced six different major divisions, with members splitting off from the parent church to begin new denominations. Five of the six divisions were based on racial issues and one was based on structural and governmental issues.

---

[1]John O. Gross, *The Beginnings of American Methodism* (Nashville: Abingdon Press, 1961), 82.

The first of these splits came in 1796, just twelve years after its organization as the Methodist Episcopal Church. A group of black members meeting in New York withdrew and established a new Methodist denomination for blacks and called themselves the African Methodist Episcopal Zion Church. This new black Methodist church prospered and grew and by 1960 had a membership of over 800,000, and continues today as a strong, black, national denomination. Then in 1816, another group of black Methodists who desired greater participation in the church, met in Philadelphia and withdrew from the Methodist Episcopal Church to form the African Methodist Episcopal Church. This new, black Methodist denomination also grew and by 1960 had a membership of approximately 1.2 million.

The next split within the Methodist Episcopal Church came not over the issue of race but as a result of a controversy over the authority of bishops and limited lay representation. This dissident group of Methodists withdrew from the parent church in 1830 and formed the Methodist Protestant Church. But the largest and most disruptive of all the splits came in 1844 over the issue of slavery when the church separated regionally between north and south. These two major bodies became the Methodist Episcopal Church, North and the Methodist Episcopal Church, South.

The final split came in 1870 when many of the freed blacks in the south withdrew from the Methodist Episcopal Church, South and formed the Christian Methodist Episcopal Church. This regional denomination of black Methodist grew to a membership of approximately 400,000 by 1960 and remains a strong black denomination today.[2]

The three black denominations that split off from the parent Methodist body represent the overwhelming majority of black Methodists in America and they have chosen to remain separate Methodist denominations. However, the largest and predominantly white Methodist bodies, the Methodist Episcopal Church, North, the Methodist Episcopal Church, South, and the Methodist Protestant Church adopted a plan of union in 1939 to reunite these three separate Methodist denominations into one church.

---

[2]*The History Of American Methodism*, Vol. 3 (Abingdon Press, 1964), 581-586.

Delegates from each of these three Methodist bodies met in Kansas City on April 25, 1939, to approve this plan of union.[3] Of the 8 million members represented by these three separate Methodist bodies, less than four percent of that total membership was black.[4] In 1940 there were 308,577 blacks in the Methodist Church, in 1950 there were 346,945, and in 1960 the total black membership was 361,388.[5] Yet, the central feature of the plan of union was an agreement to create a new jurisdictional organization structure that would segregate all black churches from white churches. The reunited church would be divided into six separate jurisdictions. This distinctive change in the fundamental organizational history of American Methodism provided for five geographic jurisdictions and one racial jurisdiction. Article I of the adopted Plan of Union states:

The Methodist Church in the United States of America shall have Jurisdictional Conferences made up as follows: Northeastern, Southeastern, North Central, South Central, Western, and Central.[6]

The purpose and effect of this jurisdictional plan was to place each white Methodist church, according to its location, into one of the five regional jurisdictions and all black churches and missions into the Central Jurisdiction that covered the entire United States. This segregated structure was the demand that the Methodist Episcopal Church, South required as the basis of union. Though the overwhelming majority of Methodists were reunited in 1939, the Methodist Church would struggle and agonize over this segregated structure for the next thirty-three years.[7]

---

[3]William K. Anderson, ed., *Methodism* (The Methodist Publishing House, 1947), 271.

[4]From a booklet entitled *The Methodist Church and Race* (Women's Division of Christian Service, The Methodist Church, 1962), 6; Anderson, *Methodism*, 261.

[5]*The History of American Methodism, Vol. III*, 490.

[6]The Methodist Church Constitution, Division II, Section VIII, Article I.

[7]Nolan B. Harmon, *The Organization of the Methodist Church* (The Methodist Publishing House, 1962), 167-175.

Methodist Organization

The distinctive characteristic of the Methodist Church's organization is central authority with a connectional relationship among all churches. The constitution of the church provides that "there shall be a General Conference for the entire church." This central, governing body "shall meet in the month of April or May once every four years," and shall have full legislative powers over all matters that are connectional.[8] By the term connectional, the Methodist Church means that each local church is a part of the total church and subject to its authority as directed by the General Conference.

It is the General Conference that establishes conditions of church membership, qualifications for its ministers, and defines and fixes the powers and duties of Jurisdictional, Annual, District, and Church Conferences. Additionally, the General Conference establishes the basis for the election of bishops and defines the power of its bishops. It further provides for a judicial system and a method of judicial procedure, as well as enacting such legislation as may be necessary. The General Conference directs all connectional endeavors of the church such as publishing, educating, and evangelizing. This central, governing body is made up of an equal number of lay and clerical delegates elected proportionately by each annual conference, and it is presided over by the bishops of the church.[9]

The six Jurisdictional Conferences, which were established as the critical requirement of reunification, meet once every four years within twelve months following the General Conference. From a practical standpoint, this new layer of organization served two principle purposes: the segregation of all black Methodist churches, ministers, missions, and members, and the means of regional election of bishops and regional control over annual conference boundaries. These were the powers and functions given to this jurisdictional structure by the 1939 Plan of Union.

The next, and clearly the most important, structural unit of the Methodist organization is the annual conference. This is the decentral-

---

[8]*Discipline of the Methodist Church* (The Methodist Publishing House, 1956), 9-10.

[9]Ibid., 11-12.

ized body of authority of the Methodist Church, and within the guidelines, rules, and regulations established by the General Conference, the annual conferences control and operate the Methodist Church. Section VII, Article II of the Methodist constitution says:

> The Annual Conference is the basic body in the church, and as such shall have reserved to it the right to vote on all constitutional amendments, on the election of ministerial and lay delegates to the General and the Jurisdiction or Central Conferences, on all matters relating to the character and conference relations of its ministerial members, and on the ordination of ministers, and such other rights as have not been delegated to the General Conference under the constitution, with the exception that the lay members may not vote on matters of ordination, character, and conference relations of ministers. It shall discharge such duties and exercise such powers as the General Conference under the constitution may determine.[10]

As is clear from this article of the constitution, the annual conference is the operating arm of the Methodist Church. It ordains its ministers, admits them to conference membership, and annually appoints them to their local church assignments. It is geographically defined and presided over by a bishop who is assigned for a four year period with the constitutional right to be reassigned for a second quadrennium. Annual conference membership consists of all ordained ministers and one lay representative from each pastoral charge or church appointment within that annual conference.[11]

As the name implies, the annual conference meets once each year to establish its programs, budgets, administrative responsibilities, and

---

[10]Ibid., 17.

[11]Methodist ordination is a two step process. Candidates for the ministry who have met the qualifications are ordained first as deacons "by the election of the Annual Conference and the laying on of hands of a bishop." The second step of ordination, after meeting the qualifications is to be ordained an elder "by the election of the Annual Conference and the laying on of hands of a bishop." An ordained elder is a fully ordained minister of the Methodist Church. Only a fully ordained elder who has served two years on trial is eligible for annual conference membership.

to appoint each of its active ministers to a specific pastoral assignment for the following twelve months. Each annual conference is divided into districts that serve as administrative areas, the number and boundaries that are established by the annual conference. Each district is administered by an appointed minister called a district superintendent.

For clarity as to the connectional nature of Methodism, one might consider the following example: A local church such as the First Methodist Church, Montgomery, Alabama, is in the Montgomery District and a member of the Alabama-West Florida Annual Conference. That annual conference is a part of the Southeastern Jurisdiction. Both the annual conference and the jurisdictional conference function under the authority of the General Conference. This complex connectional structure has been the hallmark of Methodism from its founding.

METHODIST MINISTRY

The highest level of ministry in the Methodist Church is the bishop. A bishop is an ordained minister of the Methodist Church who has been elected to the office of bishop by the jurisdictional conference in which he is a member. Although elected to the episcopacy (office of bishop) for life, and assigned as the head of a specific conference or conferences, a bishop is limited to no more than eight years in any one conference, after which one must be reassigned to a different annual conference. Duties include presiding over each session of the annual conference to which one is assigned, ordaining all qualified ministers to the office of deacon and elder, appointing district superintendents to oversee each district in the conference, and in consultation with those district superintendents, to appoint each active minister in the conference to his or her pastoral assignment.

1

THE LOSS OF INNOCENCE: 1950-1955

There is nothing more difficult to carry out, nor more doubtful of success, nor more dangerous to handle, than to initiate a new order of things.

—Machiavelli

IN 1965 CHARLES PRESTWOOD, THE MINISTER OF WHITFIELD MEMO-RIAL Methodist Church in Montgomery, Alabama, was invited to address the students and faculty of the theological schools of Union, Yale, Drew, and Boston Universities. He chose as his topic "The Southern Church, Its Past and Future Hope," and began with this paragraph:

Erskine Caldwell gazed out a parsonage window across the red hills of Georgia and saw *Tobacco Road*. Woodrow Wilson peered from a parsonage window and saw a vision of a new world which came to be known as the League of Nations. William Faulkner, as a child, walked the hallowed halls of the rectory in Oxford, Mississippi, and came to know the Temple of *Sanctuary*. T. C. Summers Jr. pulled first one book and then another from the parsonage study of his father in the sleepy, little town of Greensboro, Alabama, and saw a world with orderly progress, which made him an early defender of Charles Darwin.[1]

---

[1]Charles Prestwood was a member of the Alabama-West Florida Conference of the Methodist Church from 1957 until his death in 1977. He was a close personal friend of the author and, in 1965, gave him a copy of the unpublished speech quoted.

Each of these men grew up in the home of a Protestant clergyman of the Deep South and shared in common the influence of the church and its clergy in a quiet time of innocence. The sheltered environment of the parsonage in those years was a place of books, ideas, discussions, and reflections. The parsonage was a world traditionally free of external strife, where noble and lofty thought prevailed, and where the search for truth in a placid, secure surrounding were common ingredients. Prestwood's speech continued:

> Art Hanes romped the village where his father was a Methodist minister and saw the world as a conflict of white and black. As mayor, he presided over the city government of Birmingham when its dogs and Bull became known around the world. Martin Luther King Jr., too, shared the life of the parsonage very early. What he saw from its windows instilled in his heart the ancient chant, "Let my people go."

The parsonage for these two men was not the peaceful, protected world of isolation. It was rather the world of division and strife. Theirs was a world torn between the preservation of an old order and the explosion of a new dream, between protecting the privileges of one group and pursuing the rights of all.

If the men who entered the ministry and occupied the parsonages of the South during the 1950s and 1960s hoped for the quiet, sheltered life of thought and reflection of Caldwell, Wilson, Faulkner, and Summers, they quickly discovered that theirs was instead the world of Art Hanes and Martin Luther King Jr. These men engaged in the ministry found both their lives and their ministries defined by a stormy and sometimes violent revolution that permeated every dimension of the society in which they lived. This was not a time for abstract thought and naïve pursuit of noble ideas. It was instead a time of angry protest and courageous nonviolent action. It was also a time of malicious behavior often filled with violence. It was that unquiet time in Alabama when innocence was quickly lost and conflict was quickly begun.

That conflict, the civil rights movement, was unquestionably one of the major defining events in America in the twentieth century. But in the state of Alabama the movement was not just one of the defining events, it was the defining event. In fact, in many ways the civil rights struggle was the only event. To live through those years in Alabama was to live through a vortex of crisis, conflict, and confrontation on an almost daily basis. Each citizen, including each occupant of the parsonages, found himself enveloped in a force that consumed the state for more than a decade. Everyone was impacted. Not only those who chose to be directly or indirectly involved in the happenings of those days were affected, but also those who had no interest or desire to become entangled in the crisis of those years.

ENTERING THE METHODIST MINISTRY

In 1952, I became a minister of the Methodist Church and joined the Alabama Conference which in 1957 changed its name to the Alabama-West Florida Conference.[2] When I decided to become a minister joining the Methodist Church seemed only natural. The Methodist Church had been a prominent part of my family for at least four generations. My great-grandfather held a number of leading lay positions in the Methodist Episcopal Church South in both Houston and Schley counties of Georgia during the later half of the nineteenth century. My grandfather, during much of the first quarter of the twentieth century, was the lay leader of the First Methodist Church South in Ellaville, Georgia, and for many of those years he was a lay delegate to the South Georgia Annual Conference of the Methodist Episcopal Church, South.

I grew up as an active member of the Dexter Avenue Methodist Church in Montgomery, Alabama, during the 1930s and 1940s. My father was the Sunday school superintendent, a member of the Board

---

[2]The geographical boundaries of the Alabama Conference of the Methodist Church included all of Alabama south of a line running east to west approximately 50 miles south of Birmingham, and all of northwest Florida from just east of Mobile to the Apalachicola river (See next page.). In 1957, the Alabama Conference changed its name to the Alabama-West Florida Conference, but the boundaries remained the same. The area of Alabama north of the described boundaries constituted a separate Conference called the North Alabama Conference of the Methodist Church. There was little interchange between the two conferences, but the same bishop presided over both Alabama conferences.

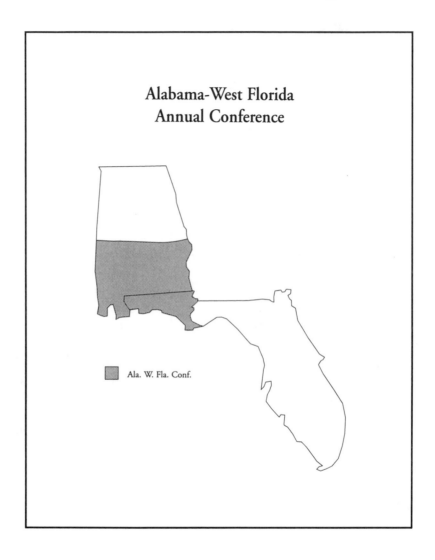

of Stewards, and the director of youth activities, and my mother taught an adult Sunday school class and sang in the choir. I also have two older brothers who are retired Methodist ministers - one in North Carolina and one in Alabama - and so I was following in a long family tradition of involvement in the Methodist Church.

This tradition of active participation and individual service was clearly a factor in my own decision to become a Methodist minister. But where my family had practiced a very conservative religious faith and most of them held a traditional southern view of racial separation, I had a discomfort with those positions. To me the church should be the instrument to heal division, bring all people together, and celebrate the common brotherhood of all men. My education, first at Asbury College and then at Candler School of Theology at Emory University, continued this dichotomy of conservative versus progressive thought. But deeply rooted somewhere within me was the determination to help bridge this great divide that separated the races and to help end that southern practice of treating blacks as less than equal. So without knowing how or when I might contribute to that better day for people of all races, I joined the Alabama-West Florida Conference of the Methodist Church.

Ministers in the Methodist Church, by their choice, join a specific Conference and receive their ordination credentials and pastoral appointments under the authority of that conference and its presiding bishop. At that 1952 conference, I was appointed by Bishop Clare Purcell to be the minister of a rural circuit with five churches located in the communities of Pike Road, Matthews, Hopewell, Fitzpatrick, and Fort Davis. From June of 1952 until January of 1969 when I left the pastoral ministry of the United Methodist Church, I served as minister of the Fort Davis-Fitzpatrick Circuit (1952-1953), St. Mark Methodist Church, Kinston, North Carolina (1954-1957), First Methodist Church, Butler, Alabama (1957-1961), First Methodist Church, Graceville, Florida (1961-1964), First Methodist Church, Tallassee, Alabama (1964-1967), and Ferry Pass Methodist Church, Pensacola, Florida (1967-1968).

When I entered the Methodist ministry in Alabama in the early 50s, I was but one of many young men who chose this path of service. In fact, between 1950 and 1955, 101 young men began their careers as ministers in the Alabama Conference of the Methodist Church. [3]For most of us those early years in the ministry started out with hope, energy, and the desire to minister to the theological, social, and personal needs of people. But unlike the experience of the first group of men mentioned in Prestwood's speech, there was no time of quiet. There was no time of innocence. There was but little time for reflection.

Conflict was the world we experienced. It was a strife and tension between the quiet ideals we believed in and a society caught in a noisy revolution. The great principles of racial equality, Christian brotherhood, and social justice that we had been taught in our theological education, were colliding with the reality of a totally segregated society intransigent against any change in its social structure and behavior. This struggle was brought to the streets of Alabama and no one could escape it. The issue of racial segregation embroiled communities both large and small. For more than a decade racial demonstrations, economic boycotts, violence, confrontation, civil disorder, and legal battles took center stage in Alabama. The issue became dominant and often divisive among friends, within families, in church congregations, civic organizations, schools, businesses, and political groups. No community leader could avoid the pervasiveness of the racial conflict, and certainly no minister as moral and ethical leader could escape the debate.

By 1968 the destructive tension of those years had taken such a toll that forty-two of those ministers were no longer active ministers in Alabama.[4] While every one of those forty-two ministers who left the ministry and/or Alabama did not leave because of the racial tension alone, the stress of Alabama's social crisis was a major factor. That dimension of attrition was not limited to the one hundred one ministers who joined the Alabama Conference between 1950 and 1955. It was also experienced by the ministers who joined both before and after those years, but who were also caught in the treacherous and tumultuous currents of those years of racial strife and confrontation.

---

[3]*Journal of the Alabama Conference, The Methodist Church*, 1950, 47; 1951, 61; 1952, 61; 1953, 66; 1954, p.69; 1955, 75.
[4]Ibid., 1968, 19-32.

The stress, guilt, despair, and painful aloneness experienced can not be evaluated solely by the ministers who left. The men who stayed also bore the scars of those troubling times and their ministries were affected in ways that are not easily measured but are far from positive in consequence. Hesitancy, caution, and reluctance to take bold and decisive stands on controversial issues were all clearly common experiences for many ministers in those years. But whether a minister stayed or left, the central experience of his ministry was strife.

THE BEGINNING OF MASSIVE RESISTANCE

In 1952, the year I entered the ministry, Autherine Lucy and Pollie Anne Myers became the first blacks to apply for admission to the all-white University of Alabama, but their efforts resulted in rioting and they were unsuccessful in desegregating the university.[5] Two years later, the United States Supreme Court rendered its March 17, 1954 decision declaring "separate but equal" unconstitutional, stating that segregated schools deprive blacks of the equal protection of the law under the Fourteenth Amendment.[6] The following year, in August 1955, the National Association for the Advancement of Colored People (NAACP) petitioned the boards of education in the seven Alabama counties of Montgomery, Mobile, Jefferson, Macon, Russell, Bullock, and Etowah to begin a desegregation plan immediately.[7]

Like a fire that sweeps across a prairie, this series of events ignited a wave of massive resistance that would dominate the state for more than a decade. The resistance took many forms, and developed in different ways over time. But the common bond that joined the various forms of resistance into a nearly impenetrable wall of opposition, was the intense determination to maintain the status quo. No one group led this resistance, and no single location was the center of activity. Albeit, one of the most vocal and effective forces of

---

[5]*Montgomery Advertiser*, 22 October 1955; *Time*, 20 February 1956, 40.

[6]*Supreme Court of the United States*, 347 U. S. 483 (1954).

[7]J. Mills Thornton III, "Challenge and Response in the Montgomery Bus Boycott of 1955-1956," *The Alabama Review* 33 (July 1980): 194; Neil R. McMillen, *The Citizens' Council* (University of Illinois Press, 1971), 43; *Montgomery Advertiser*, 8 September, 1955; Numan V. Bartley, *The Rise of Massive Resistance* (Louisiana State University Press, 1969), 82-83.

opposition was a broad-based citizen organization which came to be known as the White Citizens' Council.

As early as 1954, the White Citizens' Council became an active and growing force of resistance in Alabama. The state's first council was organized in Selma on November 29, 1954. Twelve hundred citizens of Dallas County met for a giant rally and were urged to join an "honor bound and Christian cause," in which "there could be no fence-straddling." That night six hundred men became charter members of the Dallas County Citizens' Council.[8]

The following week a second Alabama council was formed in Marengo County, an adjacent county to Dallas County. Four hundred citizens met at a giant rally in Linden, Alabama, and formed the Marengo County White Citizens' Council. Within the following two weeks, three more councils were formed at Marion in Perry County, at Greensboro in Hale County, and at Tuskegee in Macon County.[9]

From its earliest organizing efforts, the White Citizens' Councils sought and frequently obtained the support of ministers and church members. Writing about the early organizing efforts of the council in Mississippi, journalist Hodding Carter III in his book *The South Strikes Back* quotes the council as saying, "The Citizens' Councils think and plan as a group and they are able to act as individuals within the various churches . . . to which they belong. This has already proved effective in various church denominations in Mississippi."[10]

A similar approach was part of the organizing effort in Alabama as the councils sought, and often received, legitimacy by enlisting ministers to attend council meetings, to give invocations or brief talks, and by recruiting prominent church and community leaders to participate. Reverend James Love recalls that " . . . before the Sunday night that the White Citizens' Council of Lee County organized at a meeting in Auburn, all pastors of the county were asked to make the announcement from their pulpits." Instead of announcing the time and place of the meeting, Love told his congregation of the announcement request and said, "This is an unchristian organization, and I hope that

---

[8]McMillen, *The Citizens' Council*, 43.
[9]Ibid.
[10]Hodding Carter III, *The South Strikes Back* (Doubleday and Company, Inc., 1959), 163-164.

no one from this church will attend the meeting."[11] Love was not alone as there were many Methodist ministers who openly denounced the council and its activities, but there were also many ministers who supported the council and its goal of resistance.

Those ministers who cooperated with the council found wide community support, while those who opposed the council often had funds withheld from the church. They also experienced threatening phone calls in the middle of the night, active efforts to have them moved to another church, as well as personal confrontations, and other forms of intimidation. There was seldom any middle ground for the minister to take as the confrontational style of the White Citizens' Council frequently forced ministers to choose sides in the resistance battle even when the ministers were not activists.[12]

The initial growth of the White Citizen's Councils in Alabama was slow and limited to Black Belt counties with large black populations and extreme racial views. Unlike Mississippi, where the growth of the council was so explosive that by the late fall of 1954 more than thirty counties had organized councils,[13] Alabama moved more slowly with only ten counties organizing councils as of October 1955.[14] However, over the next couple of years, the growth of the council in Alabama mushroomed. By the end of 1955, the council was able to boast of twenty-six chapters with over 40,000 members, and just seven months

---

[11]Reverend James Love, written interview 8 July, 1993. Love was pastor of Pine Grove Methodist Church from June 1954 to June 1956, and an active member of the Alabama-West Florida Conference of the Methodist Church from 1953 until his retirement in 1991.

[12]In interviewing over forty Methodist ministers on this subject, this point was made so consistently and so frequently that I have chosen to list only a few ministers as representative. James Love, Powers McLeod (member Alabama-West Florida Conference 1943-1981), Floyd Enfinger (member Alabama-West Florida Conference 1951-1992), Charles Prestwood (member Alabama-West Florida Conference 1957-1969), Ed Henne (member Alabama-West Florida Conference 1952-1992), Joe Neal Blair (member Alabama-West Florida Conference 1945-1987), the author (member Alabama-West Florida Conference 1952-1968), John Lane (member Alabama-West Florida Conference 1947-1984), and many others who recalled experiences of intimidation and intrusion into the activities of the local church by members of the council.

[13]John Bartlow Martin, *The Deep South Says Never*, (Ballentine Press, 1957), 42-44.

[14]Thornton, "Challenge and Response," 213.

later in July 1956, the *Montgomery Advertiser* reported the estimated strength of the council to be in excess of 100,000.[15]

This phenomenal growth was widespread both geographically and demographically. Dissimilar from the Ku Klux Klan that appealed exclusively to the violent and extremist elements of society, the White Citizens' Council attracted and enlisted the participation of political and business leaders, professionals, laborers, homemakers, bankers, and merchants among others.

The thrust of this massive resistance was so intrusive that no one could really avoid its impact. A church congregation or its minister could not avoid making a decision about the council. Many preferred to remain uninvolved, but the aggressive demands of the council inevitably forced almost everyone to choose sides. The councils' members used every organization to which they belonged, including the church, civic groups such as the Kiwanis and Rotary Clubs, as well as local political institutions, to fight the battle of resistance. As Numan V. Bartley and Hugh D. Graham state in their book, *Southern Politics and the Second Reconstruction*, "The Councils often behaved as local vigilante committees self-commissioned to enforce racial orthodoxy."[16]

CHURCH RESISTANCE

The Methodist Church in Alabama also contributed to the resistance movement against racial justice and progress. These were still years in which the Methodist Church, like the society around it, lived with a contradiction between its stated principles and its legal and structured practice. Just as our nation in its Declaration of Independence could declare, "We hold these truths to be self-evident, that all men are created equal," it at the same time legally sanctioned racial segregation in its "separate but equal" Supreme Court declarations. The Methodist Church had a similar disparity between principle and practice. The Methodist Church's Social Creed stated, "We

---

[15]McMillen, *The Citizens' Council*, 44; *The Montgomery Advertiser*, 25 July, 1956.
[16]Numan V. Bartley and Hugh D. Graham, *Southern Politics and the Second Reconstruction* (John Hopkins University Press, 1975), 53.

believe that God is Father of all peoples and races . . . that all men are brothers. . . . We stand for the right of racial groups and . . . urge individual Christians and churches . . . in regard to racial equality. . . to bring our practices into conformity with Christian ideals."[17] At the same time the Methodist Church had a constitutional framework of racial segregation in which black churches and black ministers were legally segregated from whites in a separate all black jurisdictional structure.[18]

This inherent contradiction between the church's affirmation and the practices that were embodied in its segregated structure was made only more acute by the events unfolding in the society at large. Nowhere was this contradiction more painfully felt and agonizingly dealt with than in the internal dynamics of the church that engaged in a struggle of clergy against clergy, clergy against laymen, and local churches against the national church.

Only two weeks after Alabama's first Citizens' Council was organized in Dallas county, more than three hundred Methodist ministers and laymen met at Highlands Methodist Church in Birmingham on December 14, 1954, to organize the Association of Methodist Ministers and Laymen. The purpose of the association, as stated in their information bulletin, was to develop and implement strategies ". . . to maintain our current racial customs in churches, schools, conferences, and jurisdictions."[19] The attendees of this organizing conference came from six different Methodist conferences to form an interstate network of communication and information for the purpose of effectively opposing and resisting every effort toward an integrated church and society.

While six Methodist conferences were represented, the overwhelming majority of attendees came from the Alabama Conference. Two of the principal speakers at the organizing conference were G. Stanley Frazer, minister of St. James Methodist Church in Montgom-

---

[17]*Discipline of The Methodist Church* (The Methodist Publishing House, 1956), 702-707.

[18]Ibid., 10-21.

[19]Information Bulletin, Association of Methodist Ministers and Laymen, First issue dated 1955, 1. This statement of purpose was repeated in all subsequent bulletins which were mailed irregularly, but several time each year during the ensuing decade.

ery, and H. Paul Mathison, District Superintendent of the Troy District of the Alabama Conference.[20] In Frazer's speech, he urged the attendees to " . . . form a determined line of resistance . . . and remain united." He continued, recommending that ministers and laymen ". . . take necessary steps to . . . vigorously oppose any legislation or movement that seeks to 'liberalize' our present racial policy."[21]

Through this organization and its influence within the Methodist Church, an effective and powerful resistance movement gave legitimacy to many of the same issues and causes that were being championed by the White Citizens' Council. While the primary impact of the Association of Methodist Ministers and Laymen was felt within the church, its influence clearly reached beyond the church. Within its first four years of operation it had grown to a membership of over 34,000,[22] and had drafted and successfully secured the passage of the Dumas Bill in the Alabama Legislature.[23]

The Dumas Bill, named for Senator Larry Dumas of Jefferson County who sponsored the bill, allowed any local church to go into state court to claim title to church property if at least 65 per cent of the adult membership agreed to secede from the national denomination.[24] The bill was primarily directed at Methodist churches because in the Methodist Church all property is held "in trust" by the local congregation for the Methodist Church. Under existing Methodist church law it would not be possible for a local Methodist church to withdraw from the parent denomination and still retain title and control of the local church property.

The sole purpose of the Dumas Bill was to circumvent this Methodist church law and to allow a local church to withdraw from its parent denomination over the issue of racial segregation yet still retain the local church property. The Dumas Bill was later declared unconstitutional, but it reflected in many ways the breadth of the

---

[20] Ibid., 4.
[21] Ibid., 2
[22] Ibid., 26 September, 1960, 4.
[23] Ibid., 11 August, 1959, 3-4.
[24] *Montgomery Advertiser*, 12 August, 1959

resistance movement that frequently crossed the lines between the church, the legislature, and the Citizens' Councils.[25]

Resistance, massive resistance, was the order of the day. Whether it was through the White Citizens' Council or through the ministers and laymen of the church, the mood of Alabama in the mid-1950s was to resist any and every effort at change. As a young minister, I soon learned that these forces of resistance were encountered at every dimension of the church in Alabama. Even at the level of the annual conference which governed every local church within the boundaries of the Alabama Conference, resistance to change was paramount.

ALABAMA METHODIST CONFERENCE
VOTES TO MAINTAIN SEGREGATION

When the annual meeting of the Alabama Conference of the Methodist Church met at Huntingdon College in Montgomery from May 31 to June 3, 1955, the major business of the Conference centered on a series of memorials to the General Conference. The General Conference is the legislative, governing body of the Methodist Church which meets once every four years and was scheduled to hold its next quadrennial meeting in the spring of 1956 at Minneapolis, Minnesota. Each local annual conference expresses its will by petitioning the General Conference through Memorials.[26]

The intent of these memorials presented to the 1955 Annual session of the Alabama Conference was to petition the General Conference to maintain the current structure of racial segregation in the church. The first of these memorials stated:

---

[25] Larry Dumas was a Methodist layman. The bill he introduced and led to passage in the Alabama Legislature was drafted by the Methodist Laymen's Union. The bill was primarily directed at Methodist churches because in the Methodist Church all property is held "in trust" by the local congregation for the Methodist Church.

[26] Standing Rule 24 of the Alabama Conference of the Methodist Church provided for a committee on Memorials to be elected " . . . for the session immediately preceding the General Conference, to which shall be referred all proposed memorials to the General and Jurisdictional Conferences . . . for action of the Conference. *Journal of the Alabama Conference, The Methodist Church*, 1954, 41.

Since the Plan of Union of the Methodist Church as adopted by the Uniting Conference in 1939 is the Constitution of The Methodist Church and is the basis of the solemn covenant agreed upon by the three branches of Methodism that formed the Methodist Church; and since the Methodist Church is made up of six separate Jurisdictions, and one of these is the Central Jurisdiction composed of the Negro Annual Conferences, the Negro Mission Conferences and Missions in the United States; and believing that it is for the best interest of The Methodist Church for the continued progress of both races within the church to maintain separate Jurisdictions, Conferences, and Churches; therefore be it Resolved that the Alabama Conference memorialize the General Conference to retain our present Jurisdictional system and boundaries as provided for in the Constitution of The Methodist Church, Section VIII, Article 1.

(signed) G. Stanley Frazer
(signed) D. Slaughter
(signed) T. A. West Jr., and many others[27]

Without debate, the memorial passed, placing the Alabama Conference of the Methodist Church on record in support of maintaining a racially-segregated church. With the Methodist annual conference, the Association of Methodist Ministers and Laymen, and the White Citizens' Council all organizing a wall of resistance against impending change, the struggle was begun. For the next decade and a half this struggle divided families, congregations, ministers and the church. No one would remain untouched.

---

[27]Ibid., 1955, 57.

2

TAKING SIDES AS THE MOVEMENT BEGINS: 1955-1956

There comes a time that people get tired. . . . Tired of being segregated and humiliated. Tired of being kicked about by the brutal feet of oppression.

—Martin Luther King Jr., December 5, 1955

IN THE EARLY MORNING HOURS OF JANUARY 10, 1957, AS THE MONTGOMERY bus boycott was ending, and the blacks began riding city buses integrated by court order, a series of six dynamite bombings in Montgomery damaged or destroyed four black churches and the homes of two ministers.[1] One of the churches dynamited was the black First Baptist Church where Ralph Abernathy was pastor.

More than a mile away, the concussion and noise of the explosion awoke the family of Floyd Enfinger, the white minister of the Chisholm Methodist Church. After calming his frightened children and getting them back to bed, Enfinger made some phone calls and discovered what had caused the explosion. Later that morning at breakfast, Enfinger's children were eager to know about the explosion that had awakened them during the night. In simple terms, he tried to explain to his children what had been going on in Montgomery for the prior thirteen months with the bus boycott, and the connection with the bombing. The explanation complete, Enfinger's five year old son

---

[1]*Montgomery Advertiser*, 11 January, 1957.

turned to his father with the innocence and simple directness of a child and asked, "Daddy, what are you going to do about it?"[2]

Some form of that question, "What are you going to do about it?" confronted every citizen, black and white, during that evolving, socially-changing period that came to be known as the Montgomery bus boycott. When J. F. Blake, the Montgomery city bus driver on the Cleveland Avenue route demanded Parks give up her seat to a white and move to the back of the bus, she was confronted with the Enfinger child's question, "What are you going to do about it?" For herself and, as it turned out, for every other black person who daily suffered the indignities of a segregated bus system, she determinedly refused. She was arrested, and spontaneously the black citizens of Montgomery initiated a one day boycott that grew into a great movement for freedom. From that first moment of her arrest, until the early months of 1957 when the bus boycott, bombings, and violence had finally ended, Montgomery was the center of racial passion, conflict, and violence.[3]

Those long months of the bus boycott presented the white churches and ministers of Montgomery with a unique challenge. The boycott was unique in that it was external to the church, but addressed issues fundamental to the teachings of the church such as justice, love, brotherhood, and equality. Prior to the boycott, the issue of race for the church and its ministers had primarily been an internal battle limited to memorials, debates, and ideological struggles. However, as the Montgomery bus boycott began unfolding outside the sanctuary, the church and its ministers were called upon to lead and direct their congregations in the ideals so long espoused.

---

[2]Reverend Floyd Enfinger, written interview, 5 July, 1993. Enfinger was a Methodist minister in the Alabama-West Florida Conference from 1951 until his retirement in 1992. He was the minister at Chisholm Methodist Church in Montgomery from June 1956 to June 1960.

[3]For a thorough, detailed review of the Montgomery bus boycott, see: J. Mill Thornton III, "Challenge and Response in the Montgomery Bus Boycott of 1955-1956," *The Alabama Review 33* (July 1980); Jo Ann Gibson Robinson, *The Montgomery Bus Boycott and The Women Who Started It* (University of Tennessee Press, 1987); Martin Luther King Jr., *Stride Toward Freedom* (Harper and Row, 1958); Taylor Branch, *Parting the Waters* (Simon and Schuster, 1988).

MINISTERS AND CHURCHES RESPOND

During the early days of the bus boycott, the views of the citizens of Montgomery were not fully polarized, and, quite possibly, responsible voices could have tipped the scales of public opinion to support a fair and just resolution. The white churches and their ministers probably could have been such a voice. One of the young ministers serving a church on the outskirts of Montgomery expressed the feeling of many when he said, "If only the church leaders had spoken, the results might have been so different."[4]

In Montgomery, at the time of the boycott, there were fourteen white Methodist churches with a combined membership of 10,876,[5] out of a total white population of approximately 65,000,[6] and a total city population of approximately 107,000.[7] With roughly one out of every six white citizens of Montgomery belonging to one of the fourteen Methodist churches, it would seem that early moral and spiritual leadership by the Methodists alone could have made a difference, to say nothing of the impact it would have had if the white churches of all denominations had supported a just resolution to the boycott. However, the record shows that the churches and particularly their ministers were sadly lacking.

The seven largest and most influential Methodist churches in Montgomery had memberships ranging from over 2,000 at First Methodist to 600 at St. Mark's. Ministers from only two of those churches took a stand and involved themselves with the boycott. One, G. Stanley Frazer, actively opposed the boycott and vigorously defended the status quo. The other, Ray E. Whatley, openly supported the objectives of the boycott and within six months, he was forced to

---

[4]Reverend Stanley Mullins, written interview, 3 November, 1994. Mullins was the minister of Hope Hull Methodist Church from 1956 to 1959.

[5]*Journal of the Alabama Conference, The Methodist Church*, 1956, Statistical Table I, Montgomery District.

[6]The U. S. Census of 1950 does not identify black and white population percentages, but the popular press at the time of the Montgomery bus boycott estimated the black population of Montgomery to be approximately 40% of the total population.

[7]U. S. Census, 1950 population of Montgomery was 106,525.

move from his church. The other Methodist ministers of Montgomery were conspicuous by their silence and apparent uninvolvement.[8]

MONTGOMERY METHODIST CHURCHES, 1955

Church	*Mbrship*	*S.S. Attendance.*	*Budget*	*Minister*
District Superintendent: W.F. Calhoun				
First Church	2,332	751	$195	C. S. Forrester
Dexter Avenue	1,710	404	$105	P. A. Duffey
Forrest Avenue	1,557	530	$44	C. E. Barnes
Capitol Heights	1,206	606	$94	E. L. Hardin
Frazer Memorial	816	369	$29	C. W. Woodall
St. James	802	615	$65	G. S. Frazer
St. Mark's	590	156	$31	R. E. Whatley
Burge Memorial	470	117	$26	M. S. Brantley
Dalraida	457	174	$19	D. H. Rucker
Chisholm	413	122	$9	H. W. Rice Jr.
Whitfield	218	115	$19	A. E. Middlebrooks
St. Luke's	204	120	$9	R. S. Andrews
Normandale	65	65	$3	R. E. Johnson
St. Paul's	38	10	$2	S. D. Lewis [9]

A young minister in only his second pastoral appointment was serving one of the fourteen Methodist churches of Montgomery at the time of the boycott. When interviewed, he spoke with pain and guilt as he asked, "Where were the voices of the church for this crisis?" Answering his own question, he said, "Caution and silence was the advice from the larger church ministers . . . and their leadership was

---

[8]Reverend Ray E. Whatley, written interview, 11 January, 1994 (minister of St. Mark's Methodist Church, June, 1953-June 1956); Reverend Stanley Mullins, written interview, 3 November, 1994 (minister Hope Hull Methodist Church, June 1956-June 1959); Reverend Floyd Enfinger, written interview, 5 July, 1993 (minister Chisholm Methodist Church, June 1956-June 1960); and the personal knowledge of the author whose home was Montgomery and who was familiar with all of the churches and ministers of Montgomery during the first year of the boycott.

[9]*Journal of the Alabama Conference*, 1956, Statistical Table I and Table II.

conspicuous by its absence." He then added, "As I reflect back upon my time in Montgomery, I am not proud of the position I took nor the effect of my influence. I simply didn't want to be out on a limb where I wasn't wanted by my congregation."[10]

The minister of one of the largest Methodist church in Montgomery said when I interviewed him, ". . . Those were very turbulent years in the city of Montgomery . . . We had quite a struggle with many encounters in the local church . . . but we were able to contain them within the bonds of civility." Nowhere in the interview did he discuss or refer to what the church should have done, could have done, or actually did to help resolve the racial impasse.[11]

Leadership failure within the Methodist churches in Montgomery was but one of the factors at work during the boycott. Another factor was the active participation of one of the prominent Methodist ministers, G. Stanley Frazer, the minister of St. James Methodist Church. Frazer, who joined the Alabama Conference in 1911, was from a prominent family of Methodist ministers. His father and older brother both served as Methodist ministers and two of his sisters married Methodist ministers. He graduated from Birmingham-Southern College and held both theological and law degrees from Vanderbilt University. The author of several books, Frazer at the time of the Montgomery bus boycott was near the end of a long and distinguished career. He was a personal friend and contemporary of my parents and a frequent visitor in our home. In fact, my parents left the Dexter Avenue Methodist Church where they had been members since 1929 and became charter members of the St. James Methodist Church because of their great respect and support of Frazer and his ideas and ministry.

Both before and during the Montgomery bus boycott, Frazer used his position and influence to forcefully and eloquently defend the status quo and directly oppose the boycott. He had long been an

---

[10]The minister of the Montgomery Methodist Church, interviewed on 27 August, 1993, requested his name not be used. The full text of the interview is in the author's files.

[11]Bishop Paul Duffey, written interview, 22 April, 1994. Bishop Duffey was the minister of Dexter Avenue Methodist Church in Montgomery from June 1954 to June 1961. Bishop Duffey was elected to the office of Bishop of the United Methodist Church in 1980, and retired in 1988.

articulate spokesman for segregation both in the church and in society at large. The St. James Methodist Church where he was pastor was a frequent meeting place for the White Citizens' Council and many of his members were active Council members.[12]   The *Montgomery Advertiser*, described Frazer as a ". . . prominent Methodist minister . . . who has been a leader in the opposition movement against integration."[13] Naturally, Mayor W. A. Gayle, who was a prominent member of the Montgomery Citizens' Council,[14] selected Frazer to serve as one of the members of the mayor's citizen committee to meet and seek to negotiate an end to the boycott. The mayor knew that he could rely on Frazer and the other committee members to protect and defend the continuation of a segregated bus system in Montgomery.

About the first meeting with the mayor's citizen committee, Martin Luther King Jr. later wrote, "I remember especially the words of Dr. Frazer—one of the most outspoken segregationists in the Methodist Church . . . He made it clear that he felt the Negroes were wrong in boycotting the buses; and the even greater wrong, he contended, lay in the fact that the protest was being led by ministers of the gospel. The job of the minister, he averred, is to lead the souls of men to God, not to bring about confusion by getting tangled up in transitory social problems."[15] King was gracious enough in his comments not to point out that Frazer was one of three white ministers serving on the mayor's citizens committee who were "tangled up in transitory social problems."[16]

---

[12]The author's parents were charter members of St. James Methodist Church and personal friends of Frazer. The author is thus, very familiar with the St. James church and various activities that occurred there. Additionally, Reverend Floyd Enfinger (minister of Chisholm Methodist Church) discussed in his interview on 5 July, 1993, his personal knowledge of the many council meetings held at St. James and the members of St. James who were council members.

[13]*Montgomery Advertiser*, 8 May, 1957, page one feature article headed, "Methodist Cleric Defends Segregation In Church Work."

[14]Ibid., 11 February, 1956.

[15]King, *Stride Toward*, 116-117.

[16]The other two ministers, in addition to G. Stanley Frazer, who served on the mayor's citizens committee were Reverend Henry E. Russell, pastor of Trinity Presbyterian Church and brother to U. S. Senator Richard Russell; and Henry A. Parker, pastor of the First Baptist Church. (King, *Stride Toward*, 115).

In spite of the opposition of such prominent clergymen and the unwillingness of the citizens' committee or the bus company to respond positively or negotiate any of the simple demands of the black community, the boycott leaders still hoped for a reasonable solution. King and the other leaders of the Montgomery Improvement Association decided to extend their appeal for fairness to the general public. They bought space in the *Montgomery Advertiser* on Christmas day, 1955, for the publication of a full page document addressed "To The Montgomery Public."[17]

Highlighted in the document were many bitter experiences of general unfairness and common discourtesy which all blacks had suffered on Montgomery's city buses. Examples of physical abuse against blacks were covered, as well as instances in which bus drivers had driven past bus stops where black riders were waiting. The document then cited numerous cases in which fares of black patrons were collected at the front of the bus but the black passenger was required to enter by the rear door. While the black patron walked to the rear entrance, the bus would pull away, leaving the passenger who had already paid the fare. In conclusion, the document expressed a willingness to arbitrate these grievances with the bus company, and stressed that the boycott was a "non-violent" movement of "passive resistance."[18]

In early January 1956, Ray E. Whatley, minister of the St. Mark's Methodist Church, responded to the Montgomery Improvement Association's plea in the Christmas day newspaper advertisement. Whatley was the president of the Montgomery chapter of the Alabama Council on Human Relations, and as such, he took the initiative to invite a select group of forty religious leaders to a meeting where a panel was scheduled to lead a discussion on "The Pastor's Role In Race Relations." Out of fear of reprisal, most of the forty invitees chose not to participate. One of those invited, the Reverend George Bagley, Assistant Executive Secretary of the Baptist State Executive Board, probably expressed the fears of many when he wrote Whatley to say that ". . . he feared the publicity of Baptist people possibly appearing on the front page of the newspaper."

---

[17]*Montgomery Advertiser*, 25 December, 1955.
[18]Ibid.

Only eight ministers actually attended the panel discussion held on January 19, 1956, at the St. Mark's Methodist Church. [19] Nevertheless, those eight decided to take the following action. "First, meet with the Executive committee of the Montgomery Improvement Association to seek official commitment that the Negro citizens will drop their demand for Negro drivers at this time; second, approach J. E. Bagley of Montgomery city bus company with the idea of accepting seating arrangements similar to what the Negro citizens were requesting; and third, approach the mayor and/or city commission with the idea of settling the boycott on the above basis." [20] In addition to organizing this meeting with its follow-up action, Whatley also wrote a letter to Mayor W. A. Gayle requesting this type settlement. He sent copies of the letter to King and to the chairman of the mayor's citizens committee, Henry A. Parker. [21]

These modest efforts by Whatley to seek a constructive solution to the boycott raised great furor in his congregation. He was called "a liar, a communist, and a few other things,"[22] and the Pastoral Relations Committee and the official board of St. Mark's Methodist Church requested Bishop Clare Purcell to move Whatley at the 1956 Annual Conference. Whatley was moved, as requested, and re-assigned to Linden, Alabama, where the White Citizens' Council had organized its second Alabama unit a year and a half earlier.

Before Whatley even had an opportunity to meet his new congregation, an official of the St. Mark's Methodist Church wrote to officials of the First Methodist Church of Linden "warning of his alleged subversion." Additionally, according to Whatley, ". . . a high public official of the state and of the chief state political organization said at a meeting of the Citizens' Council that this new Methodist minister in town is not the kind of person they want in their county."[23]

---

[19]According to the minutes of the meeting kept by Ray E. Whatley, the eight attending ministers were, W. F. Calhoun, Tipton Carrell, Robert Graetz, Welton Gregory, Tom Harlin, Donald McGuire, Robert E. Hughes, and Ray E. Whatley.

[20]Reverend Ray E. Whatley, written interview, 11 January, 1994; and on copies of documents provided by Whatley.

[21]A copy of the letter was provided to the author by Whatley.

[22]Reverend Ray E. Whatley, written interview, 11 January, 1994.

[23]The state official referred to by Whatley was Sam Engelhardt of Macon county. Whatley, 11 January, 1994.

Within weeks of his arrival in Linden, and while the boycott still raged in Montgomery, the official board of First Methodist Church in Linden ". . . voted to ask that the minister be removed from the church as soon as possible." Also a number of members ". . . boycotted the church, withdrew financial support, and encouraged others to do the same." [24] One year after being assigned to Linden, Whatley was moved to the West Side Methodist Church in Mobile where he served for the next four years. However, the message of Whatley's experience was not overlooked by other Methodist ministers of the Alabama Conference. The message was clear that there was frequently a great price to be paid if a minister chose to speak out for racial justice.

THE 1956 ALABAMA METHODIST CONFERENCE

On the night of January 30, 1956, the first violence of the boycott occurred when someone threw dynamite on the porch of the home of Martin Luther King Jr. The violence continued two nights later when the home of E. D. Nixon, one of the original organizers of the boycott, was dynamited.[25] The violence and efforts at intimidation failed. The boycott was stronger than ever and continued on through March, April, and May without incident, but with continued resentment and anger in the white community.

Meanwhile, the annual session of the Alabama Conference of the Methodist Church met at Huntingdon College in Montgomery from May 29 to June 1, 1956. The purpose of the annual conference is to conduct the business of the church, establish its missions and goals for the next fiscal year, and appoint each Methodist minister to a specific church assignment for the following twelve months.

Notably, while Ray Whatley was quietly being moved from St. Mark's Methodist Church to Linden because of his involvement with the Montgomery bus boycott, the Methodist Church of Alabama in its annual session said nothing about the boycott according to the official

---

[24]Reverend Ray E. Whatley, written interviews, 2 May, 1992; 19 May, 1992; 8 January, 1994; 11 January, 1994; and also on documents provided by Whatley.

[25]*Montgomery Advertiser*, 31 January, 1956; 2 February, 1956; King Jr., *Stride Toward*, 132-135.

transcript of the meeting.[26] Neither the bishop, nor any of his eight district superintendents, nor any minister or layman ever officially mentioned one word about the boycott. In four days of meeting to report on the accomplishments of the past year and plan for the opportunities and challenges of the next year, not a single word was ever uttered about the historically-significant event that was occurring in the very city in which they were gathered. In fact, the only reference to the issue of race that occurred officially at the conference was a memorial presented by G. Stanley Frazer and amended by Circuit Judge L. S. Moore, a prominent layman from Centreville. The memorial, which was approved by a substantial majority vote of the conference read:

> Be it resolved that this Conference call upon all boards and agencies responsible for church literature and publications and pamphlets, for general distribution among our membership, to use the greatest care and all reasonable restraint to the end that The Methodist Church, through its vast resources in publishing and distribution, may not be used as a channel or medium for furthering the program of those who demand drastic changes in the racial structure of our church and its customs; and which, should these be further changed, would bring about widespread dissension in The Methodist Church in the South and would ultimately imperil both its program and its unity."[27]

On the last night of the conference, two of the young Methodist ministers, Joe Neal Blair and Ralph Nichols, were invited to attend the twice-weekly rally of the blacks in a church near Oak Park. As Blair described it, ". . . the church was packed with local blacks plus a few news reporters . . . After about two hours of speeches and encouragements, the black minister who was presiding announced that the church was surrounded by white protesters and the police. He advised

---

[26]*Journal of The Alabama Conference*, 1956, "Daily Proceedings," 45-65.
[27]Ibid., 136.

the whites to stay inside until all the blacks were gone. Then the whites were led out by a side door." Blair further indicated that

> . . . there were two white women reporters from Sweden and Norway, respectively, who needed a ride back to their hotel in downtown Montgomery and I offered to take them there. We were followed all the way to the hotel by a police car which also followed us all the way back to the campus of Huntingdon. The next day when I got back to my home, I received a call from our state representative who said he had received a call from the Montgomery police wanting to know something about the person who attended the black rally in Montgomery last night. He advised me that this would hurt my ministry if word got out that I was attending a "nigger" meeting.[28]

Word soon spread throughout the community and a number of Blair's members asked him why he had attended the meeting. Blair's experience was soon to be a common one of most of the ministers who involved themselves in any way in support of the civil rights movement,[29] forcing the ministers of Alabama to make the difficult choice between following conscience or pleasing parishioners.

On December 21, 1956, the official order of the Supreme Court ending segregated seating arrived in Montgomery. In full view of the reporters and television cameras, King, Abernathy, E. D. Nixon, and Glenn Smiley boarded a bus and sat in the front seats. They officially integrated the buses and ended the boycott.[30] Days of violence followed, but the blacks of Montgomery had won the right to ride the city buses and sit anywhere they chose. No more giving up their seats to whites. No more moving to the back of the bus when ordered. No more boarding the bus from the back door.

---

[28]Reverend Joe Neal Blair, written interview, 4 October, 1993. Blair was a minister in the Alabama Conference from 1945 until his retirement in 1987.

[29]This was experienced by the author on many occasions and was also verified as common in interviews with the Reverends L. Powers McLeod, Charles Prestwood, Tom Butts, W. B. Atkinson Jr., James Love, and many others.

[30]*Montgomery Advertiser*, 22 December, 1956; King, *Stride Toward*, 173.

A long, divisive boycott was ended. A movement of non-violent protest was born. A few Methodist ministers had actively been engaged in issues of the boycott while the Methodist Church had officially remained silent and detached. The question of Floyd Enfinger's son, "What are you going to do about it?" was yet to be answered by the church, but increasingly its ministers and laity were taking sides.

3

TUSKEGEE AND MOBILE: 1957-1958

Awareness, no matter how confused it may be, develops from every act of rebellion: the sudden, dazzling, perception that there is something in man with which he can identify himself, even if only for a moment.

—Albert Camus

CAMUS'S SUGGESTION THAT "EVERY ACT OF REBELLION" DEVELOPS THAT perception in man that he is somebody, ". . . that there is something in man with which he can identify himself," is an idea that came alive for many blacks during the Montgomery bus boycott. As the boycott ended, King and other black leaders of the South knew that they would have to organize and harness this new hope and black pride which they had witnessed if the movement was to be kept alive to expand and grow. Thus, in January of 1957, King called a meeting of black ministers and other black leaders from a number of cities across the South to discuss forming an alliance.[1] Meeting at the Ebenezer Baptist Church in Atlanta, sixty black leaders from across the South spent two days discussing the idea of a Southern movement organized to support and implement court decisions against segregation.[2]

A second meeting was held on February 14 in New Orleans, and here they voted to form a permanent organization. The "Southern Christian Leadership Conference" (SCLC) was born as an organization committed to nonviolent means of ending segregation; and perhaps

---

[1]Adam Fairclough, *To Redeem The Soul of America, The Southern Christian Leadership Conference and Martin Luther King Jr.* (University of Georgia Press, 1987), 32; Martin Luther King Jr., *Stride Toward Freedom* (Harper and Row, 1958), 175.

[2]David L. Lewis, *King, A Critical Biography* (Praeger Publishers, 1970), 88; Fairclough, *To Redeem*, 32-33.

most important of all, they elected King the first president of the group.[3]

The purpose of this newly created organization was not to compete with the older established black civil rights organizations like the NAACP, the Congress of Racial Equality (CORE), the National Urban League, and others. Rather, SCLC's purpose was to develop new strategies and methodologies, and to add another dimension to the effort in the form of a southern-based nonviolent direct action organization.

THE TUSKEGEE BOYCOTT

In the months immediately following the Montgomery bus boycott while the SCLC was organizing itself, the civil rights movement continued to expand and develop. This emerging black struggle tended to be local and limited in both organization and news coverage. But, in location after location, the movement demonstrated that the time had come when some black people were no longer willing to be denied their rights.

Two such local campaigns were the Tuskegee boycott, focused on obtaining the right to vote, and the Mobile bus desegregation petition, centered on ending segregated seating on city buses. While neither of these efforts drew as much national attention as the Montgomery bus boycott did, they nonetheless were an important part of the black movement for civil rights, a source of personal conflict for those who were involved, and the basis of bitter strife for both communities.

In the first week of June 1957, John H. Lane, along with his wife and three children, moved to Tuskegee, Alabama, to take up his duties as the newly appointed minister of the Tuskegee First Methodist Church. In writing about his Tuskegee assignment, Lane says, "After serving for five years as the first director of the Alabama-West Florida Conference Assembly Grounds at Blue Lake, near Andalusia, I was excited once more about having a congregation and being in my own pulpit, leading in worship and sharing the joys and sorrows of 'my people.' I was hungry for the pastoral relationship." Lane continues, "We were given a true Southern welcome upon our arrival at the

---

[3]Fairclough, *To Redeem*, 32-33; Lewis, *King*, 88

house, and friendly greetings from the church members served to emphasize the hospitable reception we experienced."[4]

The welcome was short-lived, however, because that same month, on June 25, 1957, the all-black Tuskegee Civic Association, under the leadership of Charles Gomillion, met for the purpose of organizing an economic boycott of all white merchants in Tuskegee. The meeting was held at the Butler Chapel African Methodist Episcopal Zion Church where 500 blacks crowded into the church with another 2500 gathered outside.[5] This meeting and the boycott that followed were the culmination of years of organized struggle by Tuskegee's blacks to obtain their constitutional right to register and vote as American citizens.

Located only forty miles east of Montgomery, Tuskegee is the home of the Tuskegee Institute, the county seat of Macon county, and a city where blacks outnumbered whites by a margin of seven to one.[6] An organized effort by Gomillion and the Tuskegee Civic Association to secure the right for all qualified blacks to register and vote had so dismayed the whites of Tuskegee and Macon county that they decided to gerrymander most blacks out of Tuskegee. Macon county state senator Sam Engelhardt Jr., introduced a bill in the state legislature to establish a predominantly-white Tuskegee electorate.[7]

The bill, entitled Alabama Act 140, passed unanimously and without debate. This new bill redrew the city limits of Tuskegee from a simple square to a bizarre twenty-five sided boundary with the specific effect of including all white voters and excluding Tuskegee Institute and all but a few black voters.[8] This bill brought about the

---

[4]Reverend John H. Lane, written interview, 18 June, 1993. Lane was a member of the Alabama-West Florida Conference from 1947 until his retirement in 1984. He was the minister of the Tuskegee First Methodist Church from June 1957 to June 1958. A "pounding" is an old rural tradition of welcoming a newcomer to the community by everyone bringing an item of food to the residence of the newcomer. It frequently consisted of a pound of this and a pound of that—thus the name, "pounding."

[5]Robert J. Norrell, *Reaping The Whirlwind: The Civil Rights Movement in Tuskegee* (New York: Alfred A. Knopf, 1985), 93.

[6]*Montgomery Advertiser*, 13 July, 1957.

[7]Ibid., 22 June, 1957; 13 July, 1957; Norrell, *Reaping*, 91-92.

[8]Bernard Taper, *Gomillion versus Lightfoot* (McGraw-Hill, 1962), 3; Norrell, *Reaping*, 91-92.

Institute and all but a few black voters.[8] This bill brought about the meeting at Butler Chapel on June 25, the subsequent boycott, and the polarized atmosphere of crisis that confronted the Reverend Lane in his first month as minister of Tuskegee First Methodist Church.

Lane was caught in a very difficult position. He sympathized with and believed in the rightness of the blacks' effort to register and vote. He also desired to minister to his white parishioners who were being hurt badly by the boycott and who opposed the blacks' cause. He was, thus, confronted with the most difficult of choices. To support the boycott openly and to uphold the blacks' efforts to obtain the basic right to vote was to risk alienation from his congregation. Yet to be silent and thus lend tacit support to the whites' efforts to continue the disfranchisement of the blacks, would be a betrayal of his convictions, his conscience, and his duty.

Lane chose to quietly and discreetly try to build bridges between the two sides in the conflict. Recalling those days Lane says, "My sympathy with the black cause more or less made it impossible for me to relate to some members of my congregation. When news reached the congregation that I had made a call on Dr. Gomillion at Tuskegee Institute, and as my stand on the race question became better understood, it was clear that my ministry had been diminished, particularly in the minds of those members who were part of the power structure in Tuskegee."[9]

As was to happen so often when a minister supported the black cause for justice and equality, the Official Board of the Tuskegee First Methodist Church requested the Montgomery District Superintendent[10] to set up a meeting with the church membership to discuss moving their minister. Lane was moved at the end of his first year because he

---

[8]Bernard Taper, *Gomillion versus Lightfoot* (McGraw-Hill, 1962), 3; Norrell, *Reaping*, 91-92.

[9]Lane, written interview, 18 June, 1993.

[10]The office of district superintendent of the Methodist Church is "to promote all the interests of the church within the bounds of his district." The district superintendent is chosen by the presiding bishop and serves as the administrative officer in his district, recommending to and working with the bishop in the appointment of all ministers and churches in his district; *Discipline of the Methodist Church* (The Methodist Publishing House, 1956), 131-134.

MOBILE BUS PETITION

In the year after the United States Supreme Court ruled that segregation on Montgomery's city buses was unconstitutional, thirty-seven black ministers of Mobile, Alabama, petitioned the Mobile City Commission ". . . to remove from the statute books such ordinance or ordinances that required segregation on our buses. "The ministers' petition further stated that they recognized the bus desegregation decision of the United States Supreme Court" . . . has involved strife, tension, disorder and even violence in some communities." But they continued, "We are bound to give courageous leadership in these times, for when our leadership is not courageous and dynamic, the forces of hate and prejudice assume control."[11]

As a positive response to the black petition, an interdenominational group of thirty-one white ministers met at St. Francis Street Methodist Church to prepare a complimentary petition of support. Led by the ministers of some of the largest and most influential churches of Mobile, seventeen Methodist, six Presbyterian, five Episcopal, two Baptist, and one Disciple of Christ clergy drafted and signed a petition. The petition urged the mayors and Boards of Commissioners of Mobile, Chickasaw, and Prichard to support the petition submitted by the representative group of black ministers.[12]

In marked contrast to the Methodist ministers of Montgomery who principally remained silent or uninvolved during the Montgomery bus boycott, the Methodist ministers of Mobile spoke forcefully and courageously. In fact, of the nine largest Methodist churches of the Mobile area with memberships of six-hundred or more, six of those ministers signed the petition. One of the three ministers who personally presented the petition at Mobile City Hall was Carl Adkins, the minister of Dauphin Way Methodist Church, the largest Methodist

---

[11]The author has a copy of the full petition in his files and it was also published in a front page article entitled "Negro Ministers Ask Segregation End On Buses," *Mobile Press Register*, 5 March, 1958, with the headline

[12]The author has a copy of the petition in his files which includes the names and denomination of each signer. A portion of the petition along with a listing of the names and churches of each minister who signed it was also published in *The Mobile Press Register*, 8 March, 1958.

church in Mobile with a membership of 2091.[13]

METHODIST CHURCHES, GREATER MOBILE AREA, 1957-1958

Church	Membership	Minister
Dist. Superintendent		A. Turnipseed*
Dauphin Way	2091	Carl Adkins*
Government St.	1425	Hugh Wilson Jr.*
Prichard First	1122	Henry Chunn*
Chickasaw	969	M. L. Warwick
Toulminville	952	A. L. Martin
Michigan Avenue	818	Tom Butts*
Springhill Avenue	816	Comer Woodall*
St. Francis St.	793	Eugene Peacock*
Ashland Place	607	O. M. Sell
Oakdale	568	B. I. Hughen
Pleasant Valley	545	H. W. Walls
West Side	493	Ray Whatley*
Broad St.	373	James Zellner*
Forrest Hill	326	Ed Henne*
Satsuma	322	James Love*
Wesley Chapel	297	W. E. Killburn
Mt. Vernon	289	Karl Stringfellow
Whistler	280	E. H. Brown
Eight Mile	231	David White*
S. Bookley	229	Lamar Brown
Saraland	214	John Parker*
Dumas	168	H. E. McCrary*
Irving-Fowl River	167	Chester Bolton*
Spring Hill	139	Joe Hastings*
St. Mark	136	Lester Spencer*

* Denotes minister signing the petition
**Also signing the petition was the associate minister of St. Francis Street Methodist Church, Langdon Garrison.[14]

---

[13]The three ministers were Carl A. Atkins, minister of Dauphin Way Methodist Church; Francis B. Wakefield Jr., rector of All Saints Episcopal Church; and John C. Frist, minister of Government Street Presbyterian Church. *The Mobile Press Register*, 8 March, 1958.

[14]*Journal of the Alabama-West Florida Conference, The Methodist Church*, 1958, Statistical Table No. 1, the Mobile District; *The Mobile Press Register*, 8 March, 1958.

Reaction to the white ministers' petition was immediate and severe. Crosses were burned at the homes and/or churches of several of the ministers, including James Love, David White, John Parker, and Tom Butts.[15] White wrote a letter to the editor of *The Mobile Press Register* which was published and which probably expressed the feeling of all those who had crosses burned to intimidate them. He wrote:

Dear Sir: On the night of March 10, 1958, a cross was burned in front of the church that I serve. As the victim of those who burned this cross, I would like to make the following remarks: . . . If this cross was burned with the intention of causing injury to me or the church that I serve, I forgive those who committed the act for any hurt or harm that I am subjected to as a result of this episode . . . . . . I would like for all concerned to know that, God helping me, I will not betray my conscience . . . I take my stand for right as He gives me the light to see the right . . . I will not do other, come what may.

David R. White, Minister
Eight Mile Methodist Church
Eight Mile, Alabama.[16]

In addition to the cross burnings, other forms of threats and acts of intimidation were focused on many of the signers of the petition. In the week following the publication of the petition, the official board of the Satsuma Methodist Church met in special called session and asked for the resignation of their minister, James Love. Love advised his official board that he had been appointed by Bishop Bachman G. Hodge, the resident bishop of the Alabama-West Florida Conference,[17] and that they would have to take the matter up with

[15]Reverend James Love, written interview, 8 July, 1993; Reverend Tom Butts,written interview, 24 September, 1993; Reverend John Parker, written interview, 11 December, 193; and Dr. Andrew S. Turnipseed, written interview, 10 January, 1994. Also based on a published letter to the editor, *The Mobile Press Register*, 16 March, 1958.

[16]*The Mobile Press Register*, 16 March, 1958.

[17]Bishop Bachman G. Hodge was elected bishop at the 1956 Southeastern Jurisdictional Conference, and assigned to the Birmingham area to replace retiring Bishop Clare Purcell. The Birmingham area included both the North Alabama

him. So informed that they did not have the authority to require Love's resignation, the official board passed a motion to immediately stop all payment of his salary.

The following day, Love reported the details of the official board meeting to the Mobile District Superintendent,[18] Andrew S. Turnipseed. Turnipseed assured Love that he was not to worry, that he would see that his salary was paid. Turnipseed met with a number of the members of Satsuma Methodist Church and as Love described it, ". . . some of my church members began to give me their church contribution checks each Sunday. On payday, I would take the checks to the church treasurer and he would give me my salary check. My salary was paid in full that year, but I was moved at the next Annual Conference."[19]

At the Michigan Avenue Methodist Church, Reverend Tom Butts experienced similar reaction from his members after he signed the petition. A meeting of the full membership was called to vote on firing Mr. Butts. When informed that only the bishop at the next annual conference could move Butts, the members were asked to withhold their funds. As a result, Butts says, "There were times in which we could barely pay my salary and the light bill. We were unable to pay our Conference obligations."[20]

Another of the ministers who suffered major repercussions because of signing the petition was the pastor of Saraland Methodist Church, John Parker. On the Sunday night following the publication of the petition, a cross was burned in front of his church. The next evening, his young daughter came running into the room where Parker and his wife were sitting and excitedly told them there was ". . . a big fire in

---

Conference and the Alabama-West Florida Conference. In the Methodist Church, each Methodist minister is assigned to a specific church by the resident bishop for a year at a time, and a local congregation has no right to remove a minister as that is a power retained by the bishop.

[18]The Alabama-West Florida Conference was divided into nine districts with a district superintendent presiding over each. *Journal of the Alabama-West Florida Conference*, 1957, p.97-103.

[19]The quote and all other information concerning Love is from a written interview, 8 July, 1993. The details were confirmed in an interview with Dr. Andrew S. Turnipseed, 10, January, 1994.

[20]Reverend Tom Butts, written interview, 24 September, 1993. Butts is a member of the Alabama-West Florida Conference, joining in 1953 and still actively serving.

the front yard." Parker looked out to see "a twelve foot cross, constructed of burlap sacks and rubber inner-tubes, wrapped around two by fours, soaked in gasoline." Parker said, "Then I called the police. A squad car drove up, and as I was outside attempting to push the burning cross to the ground, they kept saying not to mess with it, that it may be dangerous. I later discovered why they were so tenuous that night; the cross had been built in back of the local Saraland police station." Parker then went on to tell me that ". . . there was an investigation and a hearing before a judge in Mobile . . . The result of the hearing was a wrist-slapping by the judge and that was the end of it. Nothing more was done, even though it was established that the crosses were built in back of the Saraland police station."[21]

The same week of the cross burnings, Parker had to meet with a special meeting of his official board which requested his dismissal. He was moved at the following annual conference. He also received a number of late night telephone calls threatening not only him, but also other members of his family.

Almost every minister who signed the petition experienced these same or similar forms of harassment and intimidation. The most severe and sustained attacks were focused on Turnipseed as the district superintendent of Mobile. A group of about 100 Methodist laymen, in organized reaction to the petition, met at the Scottish Rite Temple to organize an effort to preserve "segregation in Mobile Methodist churches and church connected activities." Led by William B. Dillard, a layman from the Toulminville Methodist Church, the group formed a non-profit corporation called the Association of Members of Methodist Churches of the Mobile District.[22]

As its first act, the group drafted and approved a letter to Bishop Bachman G. Hodge, asking for the removal of Turnipseed as the ". . . only solution to the past agitation on integration." The letter read,

We the undersigned members of the Methodist churches in the Mobile District, being devout subjects of God first, and who believe

---

[21]Reverend John Parker, written interview, 11 December, 1993. Parker was a minister in the Alabama-West Florida Conference from 1954 until his retirement in 1993.
[22]*The Mobile Press Register*, 15 March, 1958.

in our own Christian way of life as practiced by our fore- fathers, and which we hope to perpetuate in harmony with all of the Christian leaders of our churches, but as a result of the promotion of agitation for integration, primarily by our present district superintendent, Dr. A. S. Turnipseed, we earnestly request the replacement of Dr. Turnipseed in the interest of harmony and for the continued success of Christian worship in our district.

We are very much of the opinion and have, after much prayer and discussion, reached the conclusion that this matter should receive your serious and prompt attention and that the above request is the only solution to the past agitation on integration and which we do not intend to promote or have any part of by anyone with similar views. Hoping this meets with your approval and for the hope of continued Christian harmony in our churches.[23]

The letter was circulated to thirty-one Methodist churches in the Mobile district for supporting signatures and within the first two weeks more then six hundred signatures had been obtained. According to Dillard, the letter and supporting signatures were to be presented to Bishop Hodge before the annual conference which was scheduled to begin in just two months on May 27, 1958.[24]

In addition to the letter calling for the removal of Turnipseed, the laymen's group also drew up a resolution to the Mobile city commissioners and to the governing bodies of Prichard and Chickasaw. They urged them to ignore and disregard both the petitions of the black ministers and the white ministers. They called on the city officials to maintain the current segregated bus system.[25]

As the efforts of the Methodist laymen began to spread and gain impetus, the Methodist ministers of the Mobile district assembled on April 21, 1958, and drafted a resolution in strong support of Turnipseed. The resolution read in part:

We the ministers serving charges in the Mobile District . . . rejoice in the leadership of our District Superintendent, Dr. Turnipseed, which has been effective in many areas of Christian concern . . . We recognize Dr. Turnipseed as a gentleman and a scholar who has an

---

[23]Ibid.
[24]Ibid., 22 March, 1958.
[25]Ibid., 18 March, 1958.

appreciation of the creative and prophetic in Christ's gospel . . . For him to be removed as District Superintendent of the District because of his having signed the petition regarding the buses is to set the dangerous precedent of making appointments on the basis of what opinions a preacher might have.[26]

At the next annual conference, held in May 1958, Turnipseed was returned to the Mobile district for his fifth year. The majority of the ministers who signed the original petition were also returned to the churches they had been serving. However, six of the seventeen ministers were moved because of the continued, strong opposition among their church members. These included the three ministers who had crosses burned at their churches and/or homes. All six, however, were reassigned to other churches within the Mobile district. Turnipseed stood by and strongly supported these ministers who had been under such pressure.[27]

RETAINING SEGREGATED CHURCHES

While a few men were risking their careers in places like Tuskegee and Mobile to support an open, inclusive, and just society, the Methodist Church of Alabama-West Florida was voting to retain segregation within the church. Meeting in annual session in May, 1957, the ministers and lay delegates of the Alabama-West Florida Conference were required to vote on a constitutional amendment of the Methodist Church designed to abolish the segregated, all-black Central Jurisdiction.

The amendment, commonly known as Amendment IX, had been adopted at the 1956 session of the General Conference of the Methodist Church which met in Minneapolis. In response to a growing demand across Methodism, particularly outside the South, to

---

[26]The author has a copy of the full text of the resolution written and approved by the Methodist ministers of the Mobile district on 21 April, 1958. He has also confirmed the accuracy and details of the resolution in written interviews with Reverend Tom Butts, Reverend Langdon Garrison, and Reverend Ray E. Whatley, all of whom were signers of the resolution.

[27]*Journal of the Alabama-West Florida Conference*, 1958, 100-101. Verified in written interview with Dr. Andrew S. Turnipseed, 10 January, 1994.

end segregation within the church, The General Conference passed Amendment IX. The amendment provided for a procedure of voluntary church and conference transfers for the purpose of ultimately abolishing the all-black Central Jurisdiction. The amendment began,

> Abolition of the Central Jurisdiction—The Central Jurisdiction shall be abolished when all the Annual Conferences now comprising it have been transferred to other Jurisdictions in accordance with the voluntary procedure of Article V of this section. Each remaining Bishop of the Central Jurisdiction shall thereupon be transferred to the jurisdiction to which the majority of the membership of his area have been transferred, and the Central Jurisdiction shall then be dissolved.[28]

The constitution of the Methodist Church provided that "Amendments to the Constitution shall be made upon a two-thirds majority of the General Conference present and voting and a two-thirds majority of all members of the several Annual Conferences present and voting."[29] Thus, it was the duty of the bishop of the Alabama-West Florida Conference to have the annual conference of 1957 vote on Amendment IX, just as every bishop of the 139 annual conferences of the worldwide Methodist Church was to do.[30]

On the first day of the 1957 Annual Conference, Bishop Hodge announced the schedule and procedure for voting on Amendment IX. Copies of the amendment were provided to each conference member and on Wednesday, May 30, as the first order of business, the Conference Secretary read Proposed Amendment IX to the Constitution of the Methodist Church. Debate was opened and G. Stanley Frazer, L. S. Moore, a circuit judge who was the lay delegate from Centreville, Alabama, and R. Jay Lawrence, the lay delegate from Union Springs, Alabama, all spoke against the amendment. Speaking in favor of the amendment were Eugene Peacock, I. W. Chalker, and H. Paul Mathison.

---

[28]*Discipline*, 1956, 19-20.

[29]Ibid., 13.

[30]*Journal of General Conference The Methodist Church* (The Methodist Publishing House), 967-969.

The vote was taken and the Methodists of Alabama-West Florida voted against the amendment by a vote of 262 against and 172 for.[31] Once again the Methodist Church in Alabama-West Florida went on record as a voice, almost the only voice in Methodism, opposing every proposed change, even voluntary change, in its racial structure and policies.

Across Methodism, however, the story was quite different. Amendment IX passed overwhelmingly. When the total vote of all 139 annual conferences was tallied, there were 21,148 affirmative votes to only 1,623 negative votes. Of the 1,623 votes against Amendment IX, 1,388 were from conferences in the three states of Alabama, Georgia, and Mississippi. However, only the Alabama-West Florida Conference and the North Mississippi Conference failed to pass Amendment IX. The other 137 conferences of Methodism, including Mississippi, North Alabama, and the two Georgia conferences passed Amendment IX.[32]

---

[31]*Journal of the Alabama-West Florida Conference,* 1957, 65-66.
[32]*Journal of General Conference,* 967-969.

4

WHITE RESISTANCE INTENSIFIES: 1958-1959

We say to the Supreme Court and to the entire world, "You shall not make us drink from this cup.". . . We have, through our forefathers, died before for our sacred principles. We can, if necessary, die again.
—Judge Tom P. Brady, from *Black Monday*

ONE LATE AFTERNOON IN THE EARLY MONTHS OF 1958, THE REVEREND Tom Butts left an interracial meeting he had attended on the outskirts of Talladega and in the drizzling rain started the long drive to his home in Mobile. One of the principal speakers at the meeting had been Martin Luther King Jr. As Butts drove south on highway US 231 and US 31, his mind was focused on the challenges, opportunities, and responsibilities that had been discussed during the meeting. He was trying particularly to sort through the many suggestions of the day and to ferret out those ideas he could use in his ministry in Mobile to bring about improved relations between whites and blacks. With a masters degree in pastoral counseling, Butts was particularly interested in resolving the growing racial conflict. But nowhere in his thoughts did it occur to him that as he drove, phones were ringing, license plates were being traced, and a confrontational greeting was awaiting him at his home.

As Butts described it, ". . . when I arrived home from the meeting that night, the chairman of the Official Board of my church was sitting in my living room waiting for me. Without even the courtesy of a civil greeting, he confronted me with my having attended an interracial meeting." Butts asked his board chairman, "How do you know where I have been?" The chairman replied, "[T]he Highway Patrol had taken the license [plate] numbers of all those who attended the meeting and reported it back to the local county sheriffs in each case. The sheriffs, in turn, had called the respective chairmen of the Boards in each church."[1]

A few months after Butts' confrontation with the chairman of his official board, I was a delegate to an out-of-state conference on the church's role in race relations. The conference was sponsored by the Methodist Church's Board of Christian Social Concerns. As chairman of the Committee of Race Relations of the Alabama-West Florida Conference, I and other Methodist ministers from all across the country gathered to seek answers to the conference question "What can the Methodist Church do in its own life and in the community to secure better race relations?"[2]

At the conclusion of the conference I returned home to the parsonage in Butler, Alabama. I was not greeted, like Butts, with the chairman of my official board waiting at my home, but the next day I received a phone call from my chairman who informed me that he and the president of the local bank had been called and informed about the conference I had attended. He then added that I should not attend "that kind of conference" again. I thanked him for his call and asked how he had been informed about the conference and my attendance. He declined to reveal who had called him, but it was not difficult for me to understand that my telephone conversations were being electronically monitored. Not only my attendance at this conference was conveyed to a key member of my church, but a number of other matters that I had discussed only on my home telephone also became known.

Some months later, a friend of many years stopped by our parsonage in Butler for an overnight visit. He was the director of the Wesley Foundation at the University of Kentucky and was on his way home from a youth conference he had attended in Florida. On the morning he left our home, he was stopped by the Alabama Highway Patrol about 25 miles north of our community. As a young adult with an out of state license plate he was suspect. His car and luggage were searched. He was questioned about where he had been and what he

---

[1]Reverend Tom Butts, written interview, 24 September, 1993.
[2]This question was the theme printed on all the materials and booklets provided to the participants of the conference. The author still has some of the materials in his files.

was doing in Alabama. He was threatened with arrest, and told that "outside agitators" were not welcome in Alabama.[3]

During this same period, The Reverend W. B. "Jack" Atkinson Jr. was approached by one of his church members who said to him, "Brother Jack, I am advising you that all roads leading out of Sumter county are being monitored by sheriff's deputies day and night, and the tag numbers of all cars are being recorded." His church member went on to say, "We know you have been attending some meetings, and I think you should be careful."[4]

These varied and multiple experiences were not isolated events. To the contrary, similar experiences were occurring all over the state in the aftermath of the racial conflicts in Montgomery, Tuscaloosa, Tuskegee, Mobile, Birmingham and elsewhere. Such was the climate in Alabama. The continuing struggle of the Civil Rights Movement was creating such a mounting resistance within the state that elements of a police state were increasingly evident.

For decades whites in the South had seemingly been unified in maintaining their economic and social control over the black community, but during the 1950s and 1960s different voices began to be heard. The struggle shifted to a fight for the conscience of the South. The conflict of white against white was particularly felt within the church.

In such an atmosphere, it is understandable that so many of the ministers would choose to remain silent and uninvolved. The feelings and experiences of many are probably well expressed in an interview I had with the minister who was assigned to Tuskegee First Methodist Church immediately after the Reverend John Lane was forced to move at the end of his first year because of his racial views and his support of the Tuskegee Civic Association's efforts to register black voters. The new minister said, "I am ashamed of a lot that happened in my state, and I try to put it out of my mind. I hope that it will never happen

---

[3]Reverend Thomas Fornash, who was our house guest and experienced this episode of harassment from the Alabama Highway Patrol, drove beyond the Alabama state line and then called to inform me of the details of his experience.
[4]Reverend W. B. Atkinson Jr., written interview, 24 August, 1993. Atkinson was a member of the Alabama-West Florida Conference from 1953 until his retirement in 1992.

again, but frankly, I never got involved in any of the racial problems."[5]
Another of the ministers I interviewed, served forty-six years as a
Methodist minister and said of those troubled, racially-torn years, ". . .
it wasn't a pleasant experience for me. I was like a fellow who was
sitting on a box of dynamite, doing pretty well until someone came
along and tossed a lighted match on my stool." He added, "I was there
and that is all that I wish to say about the matter."[6]

I received many similar comments from other ministers whom I
interviewed in preparing this account. They were not only disengaged
and uninvolved during those years, but in addition, they frequently
resented and opposed those who were involved. From my own
experience I know that the overwhelming majority of the Methodist
ministers in the Alabama-West Florida Conference chose to remain
silent on matters of race throughout those critical years of crisis. Some
even used that silence or their open opposition to the struggle for
racial justice to advance their own careers. But whether silent or
outspoken, all found themselves in a highly charged arena of racial
strife.

ALABAMA ADVISORY COMMITTEE,
U. S. COMMISSION ON CIVIL RIGHTS

During this time of increasing racial tensions and mounting
opposition to racial progress, the US Commission on Civil Rights
faced the major challenge of organizing advisory committees in several
states. The commission had originally been created as part of the 1957
Civil Right Act passed by Congress. Throughout 1958, the commission
was focused on having its members appointed and confirmed,
organizing itself, and initiating preliminary investigations into alleged
violations of the civil rights of black Americans, particularly in the
area of voter registration violations.

---

[5]Reverend Eugene Caddell, written interview, 17 September, 1993. Caddell was
a member of the Alabama-West Florida Conference from 1948 until his retirement in
1987. He was minister of Tuskegee First Methodist Church from June 1958 to June
1960.
    [6]Reverend Robert E. Dickerson, III, written interview, 20 July, 1993. Dickerson
transferred to the Alabama-West Florida Conference from the Mississippi Conference
in 1958 and retired in 1992.

One of the commission's first investigations in 1958 was in Alabama where they encountered strong resistance and a major confrontation with Circuit Judge George Wallace. The commission had received numerous complaints about racial discrimination in Alabama's practice of voter registration. When investigators attempted to subpoena the voting records of Barbour and Bullock counties where Wallace presided, they were threatened by Wallace with jailing if they came into his circuit to secure voting records.

The commission went to federal court and Federal Judge Frank Johnson ordered Wallace to appear in court. After first defying the federal court order, Wallace eventually turned the records over to commission investigators and complied with Johnson's order.[7]

Following the commission's encounter with Wallace and its investigation of Alabama's voter registration practices, it was clear that one of the first advisory committees to be organized should be in Alabama. Thus, in the early fall of 1959, John Doar of the US Justice Department's Civil Rights Division came to Alabama to organize the Alabama Advisory Committee.

One of Doar's first tasks was to interview potential candidates, secure additional candidate names, and to prepare a final list of candidates for nomination to be approved by the commission. During the process I was invited to join Doar and Charles Prestwood at the Methodist parsonage in Eutaw, Alabama, to assist with the screening and selection process.

Following dinner that evening, Doar, Prestwood, and I retired to a small study in the parsonage. After about an hour, the subject turned to candidates for membership on the committee and Doar informed Prestwood that he was a recommended candidate, having been suggested by his doctoral professor and others at Boston University. He first wanted our input on other candidates, both new recommendations and reviews of candidates which he had compiled from other suggestions.

---

[7]Tinsley E. Yarbrough, *Judge Frank Johnson and Human Rights in Alabama* (University of Alabama Press, 1981), p. 62-72; Jack Bass, *Unlikely Heroes* (Simon and Schuster, 1981), 81-82; *Montgomery Advertiser*, 17 December, 1958, 18 December, 1958, 16 January, 1959.

As we proceeded, the discussion turned to the potential consequences faced by anyone who agreed to serve on the committee, particularly the reprisals committee members would quite possibly experience. Regardless, Prestwood expressed a willingness to be nominated and serve on the committee. He indicated, however, that he first wanted to discuss it with his bishop and seek his approval.

Two days later Prestwood drove to Birmingham to meet with Bishop Bachman G. Hodge to discuss the matter. That evening, he called to inform me that Hodge had urged him not to accept the invitation to serve on the committee. Hodge further stated to Prestwood that if he should agree to serve on the Alabama Advisory Committee, he could not and would not assure him that he would be able to appoint him to any church in the Alabama-West Florida Conference. To the credit of the remarkable character of Prestwood, he agreed to serve on the Alabama Advisory Committee in spite of the opposition and threats of Bishop Hodge. Charles Prestwood was twenty-seven years old and serving his first appointment, in fact, his very first year as a minister in the Alabama-West Florida Conference.

Charles Prestwood was born and grew up in very humble circumstances in Brewton, Alabama, where two Methodist ministers, J. B. Nichols and Fletcher McLeod both recognized an extraordinarily brilliant mind and provided the encouragement for Prestwood to pursue his education. Charles first went to Birmingham-Southern, a Methodist College, where he graduated Phi Beta Kappa. He then received his theology degree from Boston University, where he also earned his doctorate in social ethics.

At Boston he was a graduate student along with Martin Luther King Jr. During his years at Boston, Prestwood met many of the other leaders and individuals who later played key roles in the Civil Rights Movement. After teaching one year at Birmingham-Southern while he completed his dissertation, he returned to the Alabama-West Florida Conference, and in June 1959, received his first pastoral appointment. He was assigned to Eutaw First Methodist Church in Greene County, in the heart of the Black Belt, where close to 80% of the population was black. It was predictable that Prestwood would be asked to serve on the Alabama Advisory Committee; and it was characteristic of his commitment that he accepted.

holding a series of meetings across the state to allow blacks and others the opportunity to file affidavits and give testimony regarding experiences of discrimination and violation of their civil rights. These meetings called attention to the committee members and Prestwood was soon receiving a steady stream of threatening phone calls. The Ku Klux Klan also burned a cross in his front yard, and threw stones and other objects at his home. One threat to bomb his home was so convincing that Prestwood sent his wife and children to visit her parents in Birmingham while he kept a constant watch for two consecutive nights.[8] In spite of threats by the Klan, opposition by his bishop, and substantial risk to his life and career, Prestwood played a key and constructive role throughout the 1960s, and I was privileged to work closely with him on many projects and assignments for racial justice.

THE DUMAS ACT

The closing of the 1950s in Alabama was marked by continued efforts on the part of concerned citizens to confront the barriers of segregation, and by white citizens expanding actions to resist. One of the new efforts of resistance grew out of a laymen's movement in the Methodist Church.

In July, 1959, Alabama State Senator Larry Dumas introduced a bill in the Senate to allow any local church congregation to withdraw from the parent denomination and retain the local church property regardless of the laws of the parent denomination.[9] The bill had been drafted by the legal committee of the Methodist Layman's Union. G. Stanley Frazer with his legal education and his specific knowledge of the Methodist Church's "trust clause" had provided the basic draft of the bill. Senator Dumas, a legislator from Birmingham and a Methodist layman, introduced the bill on behalf of the Methodist Layman's Union.[10] The bill sought to preserve to the local members of a church

---

[8]Based on conversations I had with Prestwood at the time these events were occurring.

[9]*Montgomery Advertiser*, 12 August, 1959.

[10]The Association of Methodist Ministers and Laymen, organized 14 December, 1954 to ". . . oppose all efforts at integration within The Methodist church," changed its name to the Methodist Layman's Union in 1959. The Legal Committee of The

their church property if the parent church promoted integration or other basic changes affecting the way of life of the local group.

The Senate unanimously passed the Dumas Bill without hearings and sent it to the House. The Alabama House did hold a hearing on the bill and retired Bishop Clare Purcell along with several other concerned Methodist ministers testified against the bill. The Dumas Bill, however, passed the house with only one negative vote, and Governor John Patterson signed it into law.[11]

Bishop Bachman G. Hodge, the active bishop of the Alabama- West Florida Conference, took no active role in opposing the Dumas Bill, but retired Purcell expressed his concern in a letter to one of the ministers who had thanked him for his testimony before the House. In his letter Purcell says, "I could not stand by and see the so-called Bill be enacted without some protest. Of course I am quite sure it will be thrown out by the courts when a real test comes." Bishop Purcell then goes on to say, "It will also leave a bad spirit in any local church which invokes the law. This latter is perhaps the worst effect of this unfortunate episode."[12]

The concerns of Purcell were indeed realized when two different Methodist church congregations chose to defect from the Methodist Church. Using the procedure of the Dumas Bill, these two congregations, the First Methodist Church, Union Springs, Alabama, and Trinity Methodist Church, Mobile, Alabama, attempted to take Methodist Church property with them in their withdrawal. Court cases followed and, ultimately, the Dumas Bill was declared unconstitutional, but the painful damage to the congregations endured for years.

Methodist Layman's Union drafted the bill introduced by Senator Dumas. (Bulletin of Methodist Layman's Union, 11 August, 1959, 3-4).

[11]*Montgomery Advertiser*, 12 August, 1959.

[12]Bishop Purcell's letter was written to Reverend Ray E. Whatley, and the author has a copy in his files.

5

METHODIST LAYMAN'S UNION VS. THE SIT-INS: 1960-1961

There is no present or future—only the past, happening over and over again—now.

—Eugene O'Neill, *A Moon for the Misbegotten*

WITH THE SUCCESSFUL PASSAGE OF THE DUMAS BILL, THE METHODIST Layman's Union boldly moved to expand its reach. Starting in the spring of 1959, the Layman's Union informed its members that:

> If we procrastinate, next year's General Conference in Denver may fix the target date for complete integration. The next step will be to send a Yankee Bishop with the duty of completing the integration program.[1]

The Layman's Union then followed that warning in a 1960 Bulletin with these words to exploit the worst fears of racial bias:

> The great masses of the laymen in the Southeast know that this policy of integration is tragic. Intimacy leads to further intimacy. Nations to the south of us have already found that social intimacies between Negroes and whites have substantially substituted the Mulatto for the pure strains of each.

---

[1]*Bulletin of Methodist Layman's Union*, April 1959.

The Methodist Layman's Union has strong convictions against mixing Negroes and whites, based on solid and provable facts.[2]

The same 1960 Bulletin said, "We think it wise to state once again that the Methodist Layman's Union has only one purpose: To prevent either the sudden or the gradual integration of Negroes and whites." With this commitment in early 1960, the Layman's Union sent a letter to all Methodist churches in Alabama, and to the 34,000 Layman Union members, announcing an economic boycott. In the letter the union urged all churches to refuse to pay the "askings" for the national church and the local conference. These "askings," formally called World Service and Conference Benevolence, were an apportioned amount that each local church contributed to the annual conference and the General Church to carry out the programs of the church beyond the local community.[3] This specific, selective economic boycott was designed to apply maximum pressure to the national Methodist church and also to the local bishop and his cabinet for their support, or perceived support, of black aspirations and an integrated, inclusive church and society.

Though the boycott was not widely adopted, a number of local churches did take quick action in response to the Methodist Layman's Union letter.[4] As requested, they voted to withhold the funds commonly called "askings" to penalize both the national Methodist Church and the Alabama-West Florida annual conference because of the church's official position on race.

J. B. Nichols, the minister of the First Methodist Church, Pensacola, Florida, and the chairman of the Alabama-West Florida Clerical delegation to the 1960 General Conference, decided that bold action from the highest level of the church was required. Silence and inaction only strengthened the hand of the Methodist Layman's Union, adding further pressure on the ministers and churches that supported the Methodist position on race, and increased the damage to the extensive

---

[2]Ibid., 26 September, 1960.
[3]The details of the Layman's Union boycott are covered and documented in an article written by Dr. J. B. Nichols, "A Tragic Era In Our History, The Story of the Methodist Layman's Union." The author has a copy in his files.
[4]*Journal of The Alabama-West Florida Conference, The Methodist Church*, 1960, 1961, Statistical Table, Report 2, Table 2.

ministry of the Methodist Church. On March 11, 1960, Nichols drove to Birmingham to the episcopal office of Bishop Bachman G. Hodge, resident bishop of the Alabama-West Florida Conference. Bishop Hodge was a conservative and cautious man with strong Alabama roots and values. Born in Renfroe, Alabama, near Talladega in 1893, the bishop had received his college degree from Birmingham College (now Birmingham-Southern College) in 1917, and his divinity degree from Candler School of Theology at Emory University in 1921. After serving pastorates in Alabama, Kentucky, and Tennessee, he was elected to the office of bishop in 1956 at the age of 63.

Nichols meeting with Hodge was tense but direct. In later discussing the meeting, Nichols said, "I explained to the Bishop that I had come with a suggestion and an urgent request." Nichols told the bishop, "Resistance to integration has been developing for a decade and ecclesiastical subversion is being promoted by the Layman's Union. The Union is becoming increasingly audacious . . . They have written the Dumas Act and secured its passage in the Alabama Legislature. Furthermore," Nichols continued, "the union is attempting coercion on our national fellowship by an attack on our system of 'askings,' threatening to withhold funds from Annual and General Conference programs." Then with unusual candor and boldness, Nichols said to Bishop Hodge, ". . . that some Methodist have even suggested that the Union might have the Bishop's support . . . that thousands of our members were waiting his clear pronouncement of opposition to the Union." Nichols then urged, "The time is here, if it is not already too late . . . to prepare a statement to be sent to our people."[5]

The bishop made no commitment that day according to Nichols. But two weeks later on March 25, 1960, a communication from the bishop's office was sent to all churches and ministers of the Alabama-West Florida Conference. Excerpts from that statement read as follows:

> I should like to refer to the importance of World Service and Conference Benevolences. They have been called "the Life-line of the Church." The World Service dollar is the money we give causes beyond the bounds of our Conference; the Conference Benevolence dollar is money we give to causes within our Conference.

---

[5] Dr. J. B. Nichols, written interview, 1 May, 1994; and article, "A Tragic Era."

. . . I have received a piece of mail sent out recently by the Layman's Union in which it was suggested that local Methodist churches might consider withholding World Service money in order to get relief from the tensions and pressures which are a part of the world picture at this time, and are troubling all of us in the Methodist Church in this General Conference year.

I cannot believe these brethren can be serious in this suggestion. If they are serious, the least I can say is I am disappointed and grieved that such a suggestion should be made and I hope and pray that pastors and the great body of laymen in this area will continue to support the World Service Program of the Church as they have always done and even in a larger way.[6]

Hodge's letter of March 25 did little to stem the increasing influence and disruptive power of the Methodist Layman's Union. On October 6, 1960, the Union held its annual meeting at Montgomery City Auditorium (see next page for invitation notice). A lead article in the *Alabama Journal* the next day was headed "Methodist Laymen Urged To Fight Integration." According to the article, James H. Gray, an Albany, Georgia, newspaper publisher and chairman of the Georgia Democratic Party, ". . . urged Methodists to conduct an all-out fight against integration of southern schools and churches."[7]

The innocuous letter mailed by Hodge in the face of a major rebellion by the Layman's Union was typical of Hodge's weak leadership as resident Bishop in Alabama. In 1959 he had urged Prestwood to decline his appointment to the Alabama Advisory committee of the U. S. Civil Rights Commission, and threatened to withhold future pastoral appointments if he accepted. That same troubled year he remained totally silent and uninvolved regarding the passage of the Dumas Act. It was left for elderly, retired Bishop Clare Purcell to testify against the bill in the Alabama house hearings.

---

[6]From a letter dated 25 March, 1960, and written by Bishop Bachman G. Hodge, resident Bishop of the Alabama-West Florida Conference, the Methodist Church.
[7]*Alabama Journal*, 7 October, 1960.

SPECIAL NOTICE

Annual Meeting of Membership

OF

Methodist Layman's Union
CITY AUDITORIUM
MONTGOMERY, ALA.
7:30 P.M., Thursday, October 6, 1960

These Are The Main Items On The Program:

1. **Election of New Officers**

2. **Report on Present Status and Future Prospects**

3. **Address by Hon. James H. Gray,**

Publisher of The Albany Herald, Albany, Georgia

NOTE AS TO ITEM 3:

This outstanding citizen of Georgia earned national recognition and acclaim when he presented the minority report on the Civil Rights section of the platform at the Los Angeles Convention of the Democratic Party — a straight-forward, persuasive and convincing presentation of the facts and law which undergird the South's position. Every great orator is clear and direct and buttresses his conclusions with recitals of truth. Our speaker is **a great gentleman, and a truly great orator.** He cannot begin to fill the engagements which are pressed upon him.

All Methodist Men and Women are invited and urged to be present. Mark October 6 on your calendar now.

Two years earlier Hodge had agreed to return Andrew Turnipseed to the Mobile district when laymen were demanding his removal because of the involvement of Methodist ministers in the Mobile bus petition. However, as part of the agreement, the bishop demanded that Turnipseed leave the Alabama-West Florida Conference and transfer to another annual conference the following year.[8] These few examples of timidity, silence, and occasionally hostile opposition to those who supported the position of the Methodist church or who followed their consciences in working for racial justice were characteristic of Bishop Hodge's tenure in Alabama. Little wonder that many ministers felt isolated and vulnerable.

Then on January 5, 1961, only a few months into his second term as resident bishop of Alabama, Bishop Bachman G. Hodge died and Bishop Paul Hardin Jr., resident bishop of South Carolina was assigned the responsibility of episcopal supervision for the Alabama-West Florida Conference for the remaining years of the quadrennium. Normally, both annual conferences in Alabama, the North Alabama Conference and the Alabama-West Florida Conference were presided over by the same bishop. But during the interim of Hodge's unfilled tenure, Hardin, the bishop of the South Carolina Conference was assigned to also supervise the Alabama-West Florida Conference, and Bishop Nolan B. Harmon, the resident bishop of the Western North Carolina Conference, was assigned the added responsibility of supervising the North Alabama Conference. Almost four years would pass before a new bishop would be elected at the next Jurisdictional Conference in July 1964.

SIT-INS, KNEEL-INS, AND THE GENERAL CONFERENCE

Tarnished hopes and deferred dreams had been the steady, almost endless diet of black youth as far back as memory dared record. But in the early months of 1960 it was different. New hopes and dreams came to life. A spontaneous, multi-state black youth movement erupted first

---

[8]Andrew Turnipseed was a prominent member of the Alabama-West Florida Conference from 1933 until May, 1959, when, under pressure, he transferred to the New York Conference. In 1973, Turnipseed transferred back to the Alabama-West Florida Conference where he retired in 1978.

in Greensboro, North Carolina, and then rapidly spread across the entire South. In what came to be known as the sit-in movement, college and high school students simply walked to lunch counters in city after city, state after state, and sat down to be served. The youth were commonly refused service, arrested, and jailed, but for month after month the sit-ins continued. Birth had been given to a new determination for freedom.[9]

During the peak of these massive, persistent sit-ins, the quadrennial meeting of the General Conference of the Methodist Church met in Denver, Colorado, April 27 to May 7, 1960. As America's black youth physically expressed their outrage at segregation in public accommodations and discrimination so regularly encountered, the elected clerical and lay delegates from every conference of the worldwide Methodist Church gathered at its legislative governing body. The delegates were there to discuss, debate, and decide the policies and programs of the Methodist Church for the next four years.

Since, ". . . no person, no paper, no organization has the authority to speak officially for the Methodist Church except only the General Conference under the constitution," [10] the debates, pronouncements, and resolutions of the General Conference are deliberate and carry the full moral weight, authority, and persuasive power of the total Methodist Church. It was with this full moral authority that the delegates in Denver spoke to the question of the sit-ins when they passed the following resolution:

> We regret that many citizens of our country are denied basic human rights. The recent wave of sit-in demonstrations and picketing at lunch counters has reminded us of such denials.
>
> We commend participating students for the dignified, nonviolent manner in which they have conducted themselves. . . . Demonstrations must be seen as a means of awakening community conscience .

---

[9]For a detailed account of the sit-in movement see: Miles Wolff, *Lunch at the 5 and 10, The Greensboro Sit-ins; A Contemporary History* (Stein and Day, 1970); Clayborne Carson, *In Struggle: SNCC And The Black Awakening of the 1960s* (Cambridge: Harvard University Press, 1981).
    [10]*Discipline of the Methodist Church* (The Methodist Publishing House, 1960), 156.

Students should be free to exercise their personal Christian responsibilities. Methodist institutions should not penalize students who do so.

All of us must recognize that the dimensions of social change are tremendous. We view the present action by students as a challenge to community responsibility—a challenge to accept Negroes in their respective communities on terms of dignity.[11]

The official body of the Methodist Church spoke clearly, unapologetically, and with conviction. The General Conference called for the changes in society which were the focus of the sit-ins and complimented the manner in which the youth had engaged the issue and the nation. This resolution spoke forcefully about an area of concern where prior General Conferences had been silent or less specific. The changing nature of the times influenced by court decisions and massive demonstrations led this General Conference to be more vocal in support of these changes at the very time that many local communities and churches were becoming more rigid in their resistance.

In Alabama this tension between local churches and the General Conference led the Methodist Layman's Union to react to this resolution. In the next issue of their bulletin, mailed to 34,000 Methodists, they condemned the General Conference resolution and called it an "approval of lawlessness." The Layman's Union statement read:

The 'sit-in' demonstrations are so-called non-violent and peaceable trespasses on private property against the wishes and orders of the owners. It is a so-called 'high-class' way of violating the civil law in any state and the criminal law in a great many states. In many places it has led to fighting and disorder. The highest and most powerful 'official' body of the Methodist Church thus puts its stamp of approval on lawlessness.[12]

The Bulletin then continued:

---

[11] *Journal of the 1960 General Conference, The Methodist Church* (The Methodist Publishing House, 1960), 1516-1517.

[12] *Bulletin of the Association of Methodist Ministers and Laymen*, 26 September, 1960, 3.

The Bulletin then continued:

> On Sunday, August 9, a "sit-in" type of breaking down in Atlanta churches was tried. For the most part it "worked." The newspaper reports indicate that in three of the four churches where it was tried, the Negroes were received. The Baptist were ready and held firm and refused them admittance. The Methodist . . . Presbyterian and Episcopalians received them . . . The Negroes won a notable victory.
>
> There is a lesson for each one of our churches in this occurrence. The Official Board of every one of our churches should consult . . . A policy and a procedure should be agreed upon. A failure to do this will cause confusion and could possibly result in your being integrated.[13]

This conflicting message between the voice of the national Methodist Church and the communication of the Alabama Methodist Layman's Union became the basis of a struggle in many communities of the Alabama-West Florida Conference as local Methodist congregations reacted to the student sit-ins, and particularly the new form of protest called kneel-ins. Just as protesting youth had done at lunch counters to challenge business's refusal to serve blacks equally with whites, now they came to church worship services to challenge the white church's exclusion of blacks at worship. In spite of the General Conference resolution in support of such youth protest, many churches followed the advice of the Methodist Layman's Union and adopted policies barring blacks from their services of worship.

In Montgomery, Roy Sublette, minister at Normandale Methodist Church, described a special ". . . Saturday night meeting of our Official Board to decide a policy in the face of a perceived threat of a 'church sit-in' by blacks." At the meeting, according to Sublette, "I tried to lead my congregation toward an 'open-door' policy, stating that I believed it wrong to bar anyone from God's house." Sublette went on to say, "The discussion continued for quite some time and eventually became heated. When the vote was taken . . . the Official

---

[13]Ibid., 4.

Board voted by an overwhelming margin to bar blacks from entrance."[14]

In Phenix City, a similar meeting occurred at the First Methodist Church. Rumors also reached this congregation that they were going to have black students attend their worship service. Their minister, Langdon Garrison said, "I met with the Board to discuss how we might respond and after a lengthy discussion, a lay woman, a Public Health nurse said, 'I say let them come and since I work with them most of the time have the ushers bring them to where I am sitting.'" Others, however, ". . . expressed resentment that blacks were only doing this to 'test us' and were not coming for the purpose of worship."[15] Although it was probably true that the sit-in and kneel-in protesters were not primarily interested in either eating or worshiping, but rather in establishing their right to do so, it was clearly and equally true that they were excluded and unwelcome because they were black. After the full discussion, the official board of Phenix City's First Methodist Church voted to bar blacks should they attempt to attend.

In Prattville, one of the businessmen's civic clubs was so concerned about the sit-ins and their community that they invited a panel of three ministers to a question and answer program on the subject. The ministers of the First Baptist Church, the First Presbyterian Church and the First Methodist Church each agreed to participate. Charles Britt, minister at First Methodist Church said that, ". . . each minister was asked to state the position of his denomination and his personal position on the segregation-integration issue. The Baptist minister spoke of the independence of each Baptist congregation and then said that his church was opposed to integration and so was he. The Presbyterian minister stated that the General Assembly had gone on record opposing all unrighteousness and so he opposed segregation in so far as it was an unrighteous practice. When my turn came I said the Methodist church believes that segregation is a stench in the nostrils

---

[14]Reverend Roy T. Sublette, written interview, 24 August, 1993. Sublette was a member of the Alabama-West Florida Conference from 1952 until his retirement in 1993.

[15]Reverend Langdon H. Garrison, written interview, 6 January, 1994. Garrison joined the Alabama-West Florida Conference in 1952 and retired in 1996.

of God and so do I."[16] In spite of Britt's expressed opposition to segregation, the Prattville, First Methodist Church adopted a policy to bar blacks from attending services.

The sit-ins and rumors of sit-ins were not focused merely on the churches in Pensacola, but on the lunch counters at the downtown stores. Joe Neal Blair, minister at Ferry Pass Methodist Church, had recently helped to form an inter-racial ministerial association in Pensacola, and had also participated in an interracial study group. Much of the community anger over the sit-ins was directed at the ministers who were known to be involved in inter-racial activities. As Blair recalls, ". . . my family received phone calls saying that they were going to do something to our children and threatened to burn a cross in our yard." Blair goes on to add an interesting follow-up, saying, "Twenty years later when I returned to Pensacola as the minister at St. Mark Methodist Church on 12th Avenue, the pastoral relations committee brought up the sit-in period and said that they hoped that I had not come to integrate that church."[17]

J. B. Nichols, minister of the First Methodist Church in Pensacola, and his associate, Reverend Stanley Mullins also received many threatening phone calls similar to those received by Blair. During the height of the sit-ins, the inter-racial ministerial association was scheduled to meet at First Methodist Church. According to Mullins, "On the day of the meeting several anonymous phone calls were received by the church office saying that no 'nigger meeting' would be held in the church at any time." Because the threats seemed very real and dangerous, Nichols called the chief of police and asked him to have his men patrol the area occasionally that evening.[18] In describing the fearful tension of that evening, Mullins said,

---

[16]Reverend Charles Britt, written interview, 10 November, 1993. Britt was a member of the Alabama-West Florida Conference from 1955 until his retirement in 1988.

[17]Reverend Joe Neal Blair, written interview, 4 October, 1993. Blair was a member of the Alabama-West Florida Conference from 1950 until his retirement in 1987.

[18] Reverend Stanley Mullins, written interview, 3 November, 1994. Mullins was a member of the Alabama-West Florida Conference from 1956 until his retirement in 1993.

I left home early for the church to turn on the lights and to watch for any trouble. When I arrived J. B. was already there. We both admitted we were nervous. About fifteen minutes before the meeting was to begin, a stranger walked in. He had on an oversized topcoat and a wide brim felt hat pulled down over his eyes. J. B. and I looked at each other thinking, "Well, here is the trouble!" After a short moment the stranger announced: "I am here from the police department. The chief sent me up here to see you don't have any trouble."[19]

These experiences were not isolated incidents but rather the common pattern that confronted many Methodist ministers. It was this type of continuous threatening tension that intimidated some of the ministers to remain silent and others to leave the ministry or to transfer out of the area. The price to be paid for supporting openness, equality, and racial justice became costlier year by year.

The Driving Force of Youth Continues

While the Layman's Union decried the sit-ins so as to stir the flames of resistance within the church, the dynamic force of the youth movement surged on. The impact of the black youth entry into the Civil Rights Movement cannot be overestimated. Throughout 1960 and 1961, more than 50,000 youth participated in demonstrations in at least a hundred different cities and towns, and more than 3,600 of these youth spent some time in jail.[20] In sit-ins, freedom rides, kneel-ins, and other forms of protest, black and white youth riveted the nation's attention on the many forms of discrimination and segregation.

Alabama communities were one of the major focal points of these demonstrations. In fact, during the many months of the freedom rides, Alabama was the primary center of violence and bloodshed. First in Anniston where the bus carrying the freedom riders was torched and burned, then in Birmingham, and in Montgomery where the freedom riders were subjected to brutal physical attacks, the nation was witness to the most brutal dimension of racism.

---

[19] Ibid.

[20] Howard Zinn, *SNNC The New Abolitionists* (Beacon Press, 1964), 16.

During these two years of sit-ins and freedom rides, America's black youth formed a new civil rights organization, the Student Non-violent Coordinating Committee, and some of Alabama's youth became its leaders. A young black from Troy, John Lewis, became the principal leader and two white youth, Bob Zellner and Sam Shirah Jr., both sons of Methodist ministers, became field secretaries.

Like Faulkner, Caldwell, Wilson, and Summers, Bob Zellner and Sam Shirah Jr., grew up in parsonages. Bob Zellner's father, Reverend James A. Zellner, was a member of the Alabama-West Florida Conference from 1938 until his retirement in 1976. Throughout those years, Reverend Zellner supported and promoted racial justice and equality. In 1947, as an active member of the Alabama Conference Chapter of the Methodist Federation For Social Action, he co-authored a book entitled, *Making Methodism Methodist*, which in addition to other liberal, progressive social values, supported equality for all. [21] Bob Zellner's father was one of the Methodist ministers in Mobile who signed the bus petition, and when he learned that the official board at Satsuma Methodist Church had voted to withhold the salary of Reverend James Love, he drove across town and gave Love an envelope of money and a promise of more.[22]

Growing up in such a home, Bob Zellner became a concerned and involved Methodist youth early in the Civil Rights Movement. While still a student at Huntingdon College in Montgomery he attended interracial meetings with Reverend Ralph Abernathy, and also attended a non-violent workshop. After graduation he spent the summer at an interracial school and then became a full-time field secretary for the Student Non-violent Coordinating Committee. Over the remaining years of the Civil Rights Movement, Zellner helped lead civil rights protests in Mississippi, Georgia, Louisiana, and Alabama. He was arrested scores of times, beaten badly on several occasions, jailed and charged with serious criminal charges simply for participating in civil rights protests. Zellner was a product of a Methodist parsonage who made many of us proud, and who made a difference.[23]

---

[21] C. C. Garner, J. F. McLeod Jr., J. B. Nichols, A. S. Turnipseed, and J. A. Zellner, *Making Methodism Methodist* (Stone and Pierce, 1947).

[22] Reverend James Love, written interview, 8 July, 1993.

[23] Zinn, *SNCC*, 168-178.

Sam Shirah Jr. was several years younger than Zellner, but like him, Shirah was reared in a Methodist parsonage where he learned the values of racial equality, justice, and brotherly love. His father Samuel C. Shirah Sr. was a member of the Alabama-West Florida Conference from 1941 until his retirement in 1981, and like Zellner's father, was an early activist in the causes of racial justice. From June 1956 to June 1959, Shirah's father was pastor of the Frazer Memorial Methodist Church in Montgomery and met regularly with King and other members of the Montgomery Improvement Association during the Montgomery Bus Boycott.

With this influence in his young life, Sam Shirah Jr., saw other youth, black and white, participating in demonstrations for freedom and justice and felt he could not remain on the sideline and be uninvolved. He dropped out of college and became a full-time worker for SNCC, assigned to white college campuses. Like his friend and "senior mentor" in the youth movement, Bob Zellner, Sam Shirah Jr. participated in civil right protests in Alabama, Mississippi, and Georgia. Arrested many times, beaten brutally more than once, he was one of the few white southerners who early joined the civil rights forces.[24] His sensitivity and insight are reflected in a statement he made to other white youth who were in the movement.

> It is a mistake for a white person to play at being black. You can't be black, so don't try. It is easy to romanticize the Negro, simply because in this period of our history, he is carrying the torch of American idealism. But one should ponder the fact that the new integrated world will have unjust and power-hungry people of both races, that the problems of freedom and justice cross the color line. Our dilemma is that we must somehow build a raceless society with the tools of a race-conscious world.[25]

The power and compassion of the words and actions of these two young sons of Methodist ministers stood in stark contrast to the all too frequent silence of the church and its official leaders. For when American citizens, white and black, were attempting to exercise their

---

[24]Ibid., 175-179; and also based on conversations I had with Sam Shirah Jr. in 1964 and 1965.
[25]Zinn, SNCC, 185.

constitutional rights and their basic human rights in the sit-in and freedom ride movements, the church in Alabama was silent. When lawless mobs brutalized the freedom riders in Anniston, Birmingham, and Montgomery, the church was silent. The two Methodist bishops of Alabama said nothing to their ministers, their congregations, or the public. The leadership cabinet of the Alabama-West Florida Conference failed to speak and the ministers of the major churches in Anniston, Birmingham, and Montgomery voiced no protest, expressed no outrage, and made no plea for human rights or respect for law and order. The church bells inviting all to worship were stilled.

6

THE SEEDS OF HATE
BEAR FRUIT: 1962-1963

With charity for all, with firmness in the right as God gives us to see the right we must work increasingly until we have achieved approximate justice for all our countrymen.

—Abraham Lincoln

RACIAL POLITICS DOMINATED 1962. A FIELD OF SIX GUBERNATORIAL candidates led by Judge George C. Wallace crisscrossed the state of Alabama. The dominant theme of all the candidates was race and the promise to maintain segregation. The *Montgomery Advertiser's* headline described the campaign with the single statement, "Racial Issue In Forefront."[1] Civil rights activists continued the demonstrations and boycotts in Birmingham, Huntsville, and Talladega, but clearly the year belonged to the politicians and to the politics of race. George C. Wallace was elected as governor and began his tenure with an inaugural address that closed by saying, "I draw the line in the dust and toss the gauntlet before the feet of tyranny. And I say: Segregation now! Segregation tomorrow! Segregation forever!"[2]

Thus began 1963, the most violent, deadly year of the civil rights movement in Alabama. By the end of that traumatic year, several people had been killed and scores more had been injured.[3] It is not

---

[1]*Montgomery Advertiser*, 4 March 1962.

[2]Bill Jones, *The Wallace Story* (American Southern Publishing Co., 1966), 70.

[3]On 23 April, 1963, William L. Moore was shot and killed on Highway U. S. 11 near Attalla, Alabama, while on a one-man freedom walk. On 4 September, 1963, an unidentified black man was shot by police following a night of rioting in Birmingham. On 15 September, 1963, a dynamite bombing of the Sixteenth Street Baptist Church in Birmingham killed four young girls, Denise McNair, Cynthia Wesley, Addie Mae Collins, and Carole Robertson. On 15 September, Johnny Robinson was killed by police in Birmingham while running from a scene of rock throwing. On 15 September,

clear why a more violent, aggressive atmosphere was experienced in 1963 than in prior years, but the signs of violence came early.

In the spring of that year, while I was working in my office at the First Methodist Church, Graceville, Florida, the telephone rang. When I answered, the voice on the other end of the line said, "Preacher. You're a nigger-lovin' s.o.b., and we're gonna see you pay for it." Before I could say anything, the caller hung up. I had received many similar calls before. Some calls had been more threatening, others more profane, but they all were intended to intimidate. But in the early months of 1963 they occurred more frequently and appeared to be more organized.

Over the years of the civil rights movement, I had received many anonymous telephone calls. Sometimes the calls came in the middle of the night. At other times an unidentified voice would utter profanity and threats in the calls to my office. But the calls I received before 1963 were always related to some specific action I had taken. What was different in these 1963 telephone calls was that they were not related to anything specific that I had done or said. They seemed simply to be an effort to intimidate me and many other Methodist ministers who had been involved in support of the blacks' struggle for freedom.[4]

One of the ministers who was also receiving harassing telephone calls, James Zellner, wrote a memorandum to about forty of our colleagues concerning the telephone calls and other forms of harassment. In the memorandum he said,

> The White Citizens' Councils, The John Birch Society, The Methodist Layman's Union, the KKK, and I believe in some instances the American Legion Committees On UnAmerican Activities in Alabama and Florida are joining forces to promote a wave of pressure on some of us who have taken an unpopular stand on racial matters.

1963, Virgil Ware was shot and killed by a white youth after he attended a KKK rally in Birmingham.

[4]My personal records reveal that several ministers reported experiencing increased opposition, harassment, and anonymous telephone threats in early 1963. The Methodist ministers with whom I talked that reported the increased harassment in early 1963 included, Charles Prestwood, William Griggs, Maxwell Hale, James Zellner, Powers McLeod, Tom Butts, and many others.

Zellner continued to identify several of the Methodist ministers who had been under pressure and the basis of his information. He concluded his memorandum by announcing, "The calling of a meeting . . . for the purpose of our taking counsel together on ways and means of facing this new threat."[5]

To extrapolate too much from the experiences which many Methodist ministers encountered in early 1963 would be questionable. Nevertheless, these unprovoked threats focused on a number of different Methodist clergymen in communities as separated as Thomasville, Panama City, Mobile, Auburn, Graceville, and Montgomery, seemed to suggest a new and more hostile opposition was emerging. Increasingly, threats of violence were heard and all forms of resistance to change were the order of the day. An aroused and angry public was responding in the same defiant mood as Governor Wallace expressed in his inaugural address when he promised segregation now, tomorrow, and forever.[6] It was into this antagonistic environment that Martin Luther King Jr., brought his campaign for open public accommodations to Birmingham in the spring of 1963.

LEADING CLERGYMEN CONDEMN BIRMINGHAM PROTESTS

Birmingham had been the scene of an extended economic boycott which had begun in March 1962. Led by black students from Miles College and Payne College, and broadly supported by the black community, the boycott had effectively hurt the business community but had failed to bring about any change in accommodations.[7]

Early in 1963, the Reverend Fred Shuttlesworth, the leader of the Alabama Christian Movement for Human Rights began meeting

---

[5]The author has in his file a copy of the Memorandum he received from Reverend James Zellner. As a result of the memorandum, a meeting was held in Hartford, Alabama, with about 30 ministers in attendance. The author was one of the attendees.

[6]*Montgomery Advertiser*, 4 March, 1962, 11 March, 1962; Jones, *Wallace*, 37; Michael Dorman, *The George Wallace Myth* (Bantam Books, 1965), 25.

[7]Richard L. Warren, "Birmingham, Brinkmanship in Race Relations," *The Christian Century*, 30 May, 1962, 689; George R. Osborne, "Boycott In Birmingham," *The Nation*, 5 May, 1962, 397; Taylor Branch, *Parting The Waters* (Simon and Schuster, 1988), 573.

secretly with King to discuss a strategy to desegregate Birmingham.[8] When the desegregation plan called Project C was launched on April 3, 1963, the initial focus was downtown department stores with sit-down lunch counters. On the first day sixty-five trained volunteers walked to their preassigned stores, sat at lunch counters, and waited to be served. When the volunteers were refused service and asked to leave, they maintained their sit-in until they were arrested for "trespassing." This pattern of daily sit-ins and arrests continued with a daily meeting to enlist volunteers for sit-ins.

One of the early volunteers was Martha "Marti" Turnipseed, a white student at Birmingham-Southern College and the daughter of Andrew Turnipseed, a prominent minister of the Alabama-West Florida Conference from 1933 until 1959 when he was pressured by Bishop Hodge to transfer to the New York Annual Conference.

Marti Turnipseed, age 19, volunteered to be a participant in the next day's sit-in where she was the only white member of a group of demonstrators seeking service at Woolworth's lunch counter. She was arrested and soon thereafter expelled from Birmingham-Southern College and forced to leave the campus that very same day. As described by her younger brother Spencer, Marti ". . . was forced off campus within hours by the college hierarchy. She had to borrow money from a friend to get home to Western New York State. She had gone from being a valued student and a member of the Birmingham-Southern community to an outcast with lightning speed." He reported further: "Marti was gone for fifteen months from Birmingham-Southern College, during which time she and the school squared off in a tense show-down over the basic rights of an American citizen to protest grievances and not be subject to punitive measures for doing so. Birmingham-Southern would take her back if she'd agree to not engage in such 'activities' as had led to her exile from campus. She would only go back, she said, if such unconstitutional and unchristian qualifications were lifted. Finally, Birmingham-Southern blinked first. She was readmitted on her own terms in the fall of 1964."[9]

---

[8]Martin Luther King Jr., *Why We Can't Wait* (Harper and Row, 1963), 47.

[9]Reverend A. Spencer Turnipseed, from a speech given to Southeastern Jurisdictional Historical Society, 12 July, 1995, meeting at Dexter Avenue United Methodist Church, Montgomery, Alabama, and also from an interview with Reverend

The weeks of sit-in demonstrations continued daily in Birmingham, and then on Good Friday, April 12, King and Abernathy, dressed in work clothes, and joined by about 50 other protesters, marched to the downtown district where Chief of Police "Bull" Connor ordered their arrest.[10]

On the day of King's arrest, the local newspaper published a public statement directed to King and signed by eight of the most prestigious white clergymen in Alabama.[11] Bishop Paul Hardin Jr., the Methodist bishop of the Alabama-West Florida Conference, and Bishop Nolan B. Harmon, the Methodist bishop of the North Alabama Conference, were joined by bishops of the Episcopal Church, the Synod Moderator of the Presbyterian Church, the pastor of Birmingham's largest Baptist church, and the rabbi of the Jewish Temple. They all put the weight of their offices against the efforts of the demonstrations which they charged as being ". . . directed and led in part by outsiders." The statement also charged the demonstrators with ". . . such actions as to incite hatred and violence."

Nowhere did Hardin or any of the other religious leaders condemn the segregation and discrimination that denied basic human and constitutional rights to Birmingham's blacks. Neither did they express any concern over the beatings and bombings which had occurred in the recent past in Birmingham. They simply commended the community, the news media, and law enforcement officials and ". . . strongly urged our own Negro community to withdraw support from these demonstrations."[12] Notably, the eight prominent clergymen who wrote their public letter criticizing King and the other black demonstrators were totally silent two months later when Governor Wallace defied both a federal court order and a federal injunction by standing in the schoolhouse door to block the integration of the University of Alabama.

Spencer Turnipseed, 8 May, 1997.

[10]*The Birmingham News*, 13 April, 1963; Adam Fairclough, *To Redeem The Soul of America, The Southern Christian Leadership Conference and Martin Luther King Jr.* (University of Georgia Press, 1987), 121-122; David L. Lewis, *King, A Critical Biography* (Praeger Publishers, 1970), 183-184.

[11]*Letter From Birmingham City Jail*, a booklet published in May 1963, by American Friends Service Committee, 15; *The Birmingham News*, 13 April, 1963.

[12]*Letter From Birmingham*, 15.

King was in jail when the clergymen's letter was published in the local newspaper. His response, *Letter From Birmingham City Jail*, was dated April 16, 1963, and was written from his jail cell on scraps of paper and on the margins of the very newspaper from which he read the published clergymen's statement. "My dear Fellow Clergymen," he began. "While confined here in the Birmingham City Jail, I came across your recent statement calling our present activities 'unwise and untimely.'"[13] King expressed disappointment with the white church in not opening its doors or supporting the aspirations of blacks for justice and equality. He further chided these clergymen for commending the community and law enforcement officials while failing to commend the 'sublime courage' of the demonstrators.[14]

Surely, Hardin and the other religious leaders did not intend to encourage, aid or comfort Connor and the other leaders of white resistance. Nevertheless, the result of their criticism of the Birmingham demonstrators seemed to do precisely that. Just two weeks after the clergymen published their critical statement in the *Birmingham News*, Connor and his police turned high pressure fire hoses and police dogs on the demonstrators.

The daily protests continued and early in May the encounters between the black protesters and the fire hoses and dogs of Connor became increasingly violent. A negotiated settlement in mid-May was followed by a series of night bombings, a national television address by President Kennedy, the sending of three thousand federal troops to Birmingham, and a defiant Governor Wallace challenging President Kennedy's actions. In this highly charged atmosphere, the Annual Conference of the Alabama-West Florida Conference of the Methodist Church convened.

METHODISTS' 1963 ANNUAL CONFERENCE

From May 28 to May 31, 1963, the annual meeting of the Alabama-West Florida Conference was held at Huntingdon College in Montgomery, Alabama. In the racially troubled times in which this conference was held, it is noteworthy that a report calling for positive

---

[13]Ibid., 2; Lewis, *King*, 187.
[14]*Letter From Birmingham*, 7-14.

and constructive solutions to the racial conflict was passed. As conference chairman of the Division of Race Relations, I had drafted a resolution called "A Call To Christian Thought And Conduct "as a part of the report of the Board of Christian Social Concerns. The resolution began:

A Call to Christian Thought and Conduct

The decisions of the Supreme Court of the United States relative to segregation have made necessary far reaching and often difficult community re-adjustments throughout the nation. Communities within our Conference are now confronting or will soon confront this difficult re-adjustment. As Methodist Christians we must relate our Christian faith to this vital issue upon which many of our people are divided. We do not pretend to know all the answers. Nevertheless, we do know the ultimate spirit in which all problems of human relations must be solved.[15]

The seven-point report called upon all Christians to uphold the law, repudiate racial hatred and violence, support freedom and equality for all, and apply compassion and understanding to those with whom we differ. Even though this resolution was quite moderate in its call for recognition of basic human rights to all humanity, it was considered radical at the time. A spirited, emotional, and potentially divisive debate followed with strong opposition against the idea of readjustments in our communities. Concerned at the pointed rhetoric and passionate feelings on the debate floor, Bishop Paul Hardin Jr. stepped aside from his role as presiding officer of the conference and asked for a point of personal privilege. Stepping to the lectern, he implored the delegates to exhibit ". . . a spirit of unity among all regardless of their personal convictions in the manner of Social Concerns."[16] Dissenters attempted to change and even delete this resolution from the conference report, but when the vote on the report was taken, it passed by the margin of 156 for and 116 against.[17]

---

[15]*Journal of the Alabama-West Florida Conference, The Methodist Church,* 1963, 154-155.
[16]Ibid.
[17]Ibid., 93.

Methodist Conference on Human Relations

Two months after the adjournment of the 1963 Annual Confer-
ence, and on the very eve of the historic March on Washington, the
Second Methodist Conference on Human Relations convened at the
Hilton Hotel in Chicago, August 26-30, 1963. Reverend James Love
and I were the official delegates from the Alabama-West Florida
Conference. We joined Methodist ministers from all across America
for the purpose of ". . . bringing about racial inclusiveness in The
Methodist Church and . . . in the communities in which it serves."[18]
Three questions were to be addressed at the conference:

1) Where is The Methodist Church currently in its structure and
program in regard to race relations?

2) What are the immediate goals toward which The Methodist
Church should move in race relations?

3) How can The Methodist Church make the greatest progress
toward these goals?[19]

Many nationally-known leaders were on the conference program,
but the highlight of the conference came on Tuesday, August 27, when
Martin Luther King Jr. addressed the conference. Speaking on the
subject, "The Role Of The Church In This Period Of Social Change,"
King began by saying, "Segregation is on its deathbed and the only
question confronting the church and the nation is how costly and
bloody they will make its funeral." He shortly followed that statement
by saying, "At 11:00 o'clock on Sunday morning when we sing 'In
Christ there is no East or West,' we are in the most totally segregated
hour of the week, and the most segregated schools in America are the
church schools."[20]

---

[18]This statement was the officially stated purpose of the conference and was
printed on all the materials of the delegates and announced to the total church
through its literature.

[19]These questions were printed on the cover of the conference materials given to
each delegate. The author has copies in his files.

[20]These quotes are from the notes taken by the author at the conference.

Following his address, the delegates met in small discussion groups to prepare and recommend "suggestions for action" based on King's comments and the conference purpose. As a discussion leader, it was my good fortune that King joined our group to participate in the discussion. In the few minutes we had before the group discussions began, I spoke with King and asked him about his hopes for the March on Washington scheduled to take place the next day.

Surprisingly, he was concerned and apprehensive about the size of the turnout. Such a high-profile national event had never been staged by the civil rights organizations, and how many people would respond and come to march in Washington was unknown. Broad support from all sections of America was important and as the time approached, King was concerned. He made no reference to himself nor did he give any hint of the remarks he would say in Washington.

The next day, Love and I skipped a portion of the conference to listen to King's speech on television. I had heard and met King on previous occasions, but nothing prepared me for the emotional impact of his "I Have A Dream" speech. Not ordinarily moved to tears, I sat with tears streaming down my face as I saw more than 200,000 marchers standing before the Lincoln Memorial listening to one of the most poignantly expressed dreams ever uttered.

INTEGRATING ALABAMA'S PUBLIC SCHOOLS

The March on Washington had barely ended when a new crisis developed in Alabama. For nine years Alabama had resisted public school integration and had successfully blocked every effort made to implement the 1954 US Supreme Court school desegregation decision. State after state, including Mississippi, had yielded to court orders and integrated some of their schools. But Alabama resisted.

It was not until June 1963, following Governor George Wallace's dramatic "stand in the schoolhouse door," that the University of Alabama was finally integrated and the first crack appeared in Alabama's wall of school segregation. Then two months later the wall cracked wider. In a series of separate federal court rulings, Alabama was ordered, for the first time, to integrate the public schools below the university level.[21]

In Mobile, Birmingham, and Tuskegee, schools were ordered by the federal court to integrate, and in Huntsville the local school board had voluntarily decided to begin desegregating their schools. Murphy High School in Mobile was ordered to admit two blacks on September 6. Birmingham was ordered to desegregate their schools on September 3. Huntsville had scheduled their desegregation to begin on September 3; and Tuskegee High School was under order to admit thirteen black students on September 2. Since the high school in Tuskegee was to be the first one integrated, this town became the immediate new battleground of resistance.

Tuskegee had been a town living in racial tension and conflict for many years, but in the early months of 1963 three unrelated events occurred that were destined to collide on September 2nd in this small county seat town. First, Governor Wallace was inaugurated after having pledged to the voters of Alabama that when ". . . schools are threatened with integration . . . I shall resist any . . . federal court order even to the point of standing in the schoolhouse door in person, if necessary."[22]

Second, in the spring of 1963, Detroit Lee and his wife, a black couple, entered a lawsuit requesting Tuskegee High School to admit their sons, Anthony and Henry, as well as other blacks.[23] In May of that same year, the third event occurred when Ennis Sellers, the minister of the First Methodist Church of Tuskegee, was elected president of the Tuskegee High School Parent Teachers Association.[24]

For Sellers, the difficulties he encountered in his church began on the evening of August 29 when, as president of the PTA, he chaired a

---

[21]Jack Bass, *Taming The Storm* (Doubleday, 1993), 208-209; Tinsley E. Yarbrough, *Judge Frank Johnson and Human Rights in Alabama* (University of Alabama Press, 1981), 92-93; Robert J. Norrell, *Reaping The Whirlwind* (Alfred A Knopf, 1985), 137; *Time*, 13 September, 1963, 26-27.

[22]George C. Wallace, 1962 campaign speech *Hear Me Out* (Drake House Publishers, 1968), 130; *Montgomery Advertiser*, 4 March 1962, 11 March, 1962; Jones, *Wallace Story*, 37.

[23]Frank Sikora, *The Judge, The Life and Opinions of Alabama's Frank M. Johnson Jr.* (The Black Belt Press, 1992), 168; Bass, *Taming*, 208.

[24]Norrell, *Reaping*, 138.

community meeting to discuss the scheduled school integration. Sellers, in his fourth year as the minister of Tuskegee's First Methodist Church, openly supported school integration and other black aspirations. Nonetheless, he was respected, even if not always approved of, by his members.

At that meeting, the school board president, the superintendent of education, the principal of Tuskegee High School, and Sellers attempted to explain to the 400 white citizens who had gathered, the plan to comply with Judge Johnson's court order to admit thirteen black students to Tuskegee High School. As the meeting progressed, anger and tension mounted. The crowd demanded that school opening be delayed, that Governor Wallace be consulted, and that the community take a stand against integration.[25]

Tuskegee's school crisis only worsened in the weeks and months that followed. On September 2nd, in defiance of Judge Johnson's court order, Wallace sent 200 state troopers to close the school and prevent anyone from entering. When the school finally opened a week later, all the white students boycotted Tuskegee High and enrolled in a private academy with the support and financial assistance of the governor. By year end, with only the thirteen black students in attendance, Wallace closed Tuskegee High School.[26]

During these months of crisis, Sellers faced numerous challenges from his congregation and found himself increasingly at odds with many of his church members. One member proposed to the church's official board that the church facilities be used for the new private school. Another member proposed placing ushers as guards outside the church door each Sunday to prevent any black from entering and then locking the doors once all the members were inside.

---

[25]The author is a personal friend of Reverend Ennis Sellers and in 1968 was invited by Sellers to conduct Holy Week services at the Ashland Place Methodist Church in Mobile where Sellers was minister. During the week, the details of the Tuskegee desegregation crisis were discussed and the author made notes of Seller's account. Additionally, in 1964 Mr. Sellers wrote an unpublished manuscript of the Tuskegee events, entitled "Tuskegee, The Methodist Church and School Integration." Pertinent information from this manuscript concerning Sellers and the Methodist Church is included in Norrell, *Reaping*, 138-157).

[26]Norrell, *Reaping*, 144-145; Bass, *Taming*, 208-209.

Sellers prevented these proposals from being adopted and implemented, but the cost was severe. Attendance dropped dramatically, contributions and financial pledges were withheld, numerous members withdrew their support from the church, and Sellers' effectiveness was substantially diminished. A few months later at the next annual conference, the bishop moved Sellers.

A minister "more acceptable" to the membership was assigned to the First Methodist Church of Tuskegee. One of the very first actions of the official board under the new minister was to adopt a policy to place ushers as guards outside the church doors each Sunday to assure no blacks would be admitted, and then to lock the door after all members were inside. This "closed door policy" remained in effect for the next five years.[27]

THE DUMAS ACT AND A METHODIST WITHDRAWAL

Twenty-one miles south of Tuskegee on highway US 29 is the small, rural, Black Belt town of Union Springs. It had been spared the years of racial turmoil experienced by its neighboring community of Tuskegee, but its white citizens, nonetheless, had reached a point of defiant anger. Whether some specific event or just the accumulation of many events triggered this anger into action is not clear. But in November, 1963, the official board of the Union Springs Methodist Church voted unanimously (21 to 0) to withdraw from the Methodist Church and use the provisions of the Dumas Act to retain the church property.

The official board then scheduled a church conference for Sunday, November 24, to provide the entire church membership with the opportunity to vote on the withdrawal proposal (the Dumas Act enacted by the Alabama legislature in 1959 provided that with a 65 percent vote of adult members, a local church might withdraw from the parent denomination and retain all church property).

In a statement prepared by representatives of those members seeking to withdraw, and published in the *Union Springs Herald*, the reasons given for withdrawing from the Methodist Church were "1) trends in the Methodist Church were not in line with our thinking; 2)

---

[27]Sellers, see footnote #26.

condonement of the Negro March on Washington by the Methodist Council of Bishops; and 3) unfavorable trends in writings appearing in various church publications."[28] The minister of the Union Springs Methodist Church, Haywood Scott, encouraged and supported the withdrawal. When he was asked for his reasons, he said, "I have been disturbed for some time over the liberal trend in the Methodist Church, not only because of the race issue but also because of a dictatorship in hierarchy." Scott then added, ". . . another cause for alarm to me is the National Council of Churches' complete disregard for the Southern way of life."[29]

When word reached Bishop Paul Hardin Jr. of the November 24th scheduled meeting of the membership of the Union Springs Methodist Church, the bishop discussed the urgency and critical importance of the matter with Reverend Torrence Maxey, the district superintendent of the Troy District in which the Union Springs church was located. The bishop next called Scott and the church lay leader of the Union Springs church and ". . . urged that the proposed action not be taken."[30]

Hardin then issued a statement which was mailed to all ministers in the Alabama-West Florida Conference providing detailed information on the Union Springs Methodist Church. In part the statement read:

> On Sunday, November 24, 1963, Mr. Maxey as a personal representative of Bishop Hardin and The Methodist Church, sought to attend the 'church conference.' Bishop Hardin had given Mr. Maxey a statement to make and Mr. Maxey had one of his own. Before the service Mr. Scott and several laymen were made aware of Mr. Maxey's desire to make these statements. They said that the Superintendent could not be present, because they wanted the proposal to pass without any 'trouble.'

---

[28]*The Union Springs Herald*, 27 November 1963.

[29]*Montgomery Advertiser*, 27 November 1963.

[30]From a four page statement prepared by Bishop Paul Hardin Jr., and Reverend Torrence Maxey and submitted for approval to the district superintendents of the Alabama-West Florida Conference. The statement was then mailed to all ministers of the Conference and the author has a copy in his files.

They also said that if the Bishop had come, he, too, would have been excluded from the meeting. When Mr. Maxey did seek to attend the meeting, he was ejected from the church by several men. Mr. Maxey explained that he had a right and duty to be there as a representative of the presiding Bishop. Mr. Scott personally informed Mr. Maxey that he would not be able to make a statement.

. . . from the vestibule of the church, Mr. Maxey heard Mr. Scott open the meeting and give a fervent plea for the church to withdraw . . . There were motions for a delay and also for a secret ballot. Both were defeated. The motion to withdraw carried by a vote of 97 to 12 . . . Then the church voted to affiliate with the Southern Methodist Church.[31]

The shock waves of the withdrawal of the Union Springs Methodist Church reverberated across the Alabama-West Florida Conference. The story was not only carried on page one of the daily newspapers in Mobile, Birmingham, Dothan, Montgomery, Selma, and elsewhere, but it was also carried in county seat weekly newspapers all over the state. From Brundidge to Abbeville, from Fort Deposit to Greenville, from Andalusia to Foley, from Centreville to Linden, from Marion to Ozark, the headlines featured the Union Springs withdrawal from the Methodist Church over the issue of race.[32]

Knowing the potential for widespread revolt and division was real, Hardin and his cabinet acted quickly and decisively. On December 18th, Hardin notified Scott that his ministerial privileges were suspended. The bishop next turned to the court. A suit was filed on February 24th before Circuit Judge Jack Wallace, the brother of Governor George Wallace. When the case finally came to trial in June 1966, Judge Jack Wallace ruled against the Methodist Church using the Dumas Act as the basis of his decision. The Methodist Church appealed his decision.

In the meantime, two separate congregations met each week for worship services. The majority that had withdrawn and aligned themselves with the Southern Methodist Church continued to worship

---

[31]Hardin, Maxey, see footnote #30; The Southern Methodist Church was a small denomination with headquarters located in Orangeburg, South Carolina.

[32]The author has copies of newspaper articles from most of the listed communities.

in the church facilities, and Scott remained as their pastor and continued living in the parsonage.

A small group of about thirty loyal Methodists, who refused to withdraw, met each Sunday for worship in the Masonic building and then later moved to the ublic library. Their groupgrew to fifty-six by the time the Alabama Supreme Court rendered its historic decision.

The Alabama Supreme Court declared on September 4, 1969 that Alabama Code No. 79, commonly known as the Dumas Act, was unconstitutional and ruled in favor of the Methodist Church in the Union Springs church property case. The unanimous ruling, signed by all six justices said, "We do not think it can be doubted that the decisions of the Supreme Court of the United States hold that a statue such as Act No. 79 violates the First Amendment guarantee of religious freedom . . . we hold that Act No. 79 is unconstitutional and invalid as applied in the instant case."[33]

The legal battle had ended. The Methodist Church had prevailed. But the scars and bitterness of the conflict over local control of church property and over the complex issue of race would take years to heal. By the time of the court decision, Bishop Paul Hardin Jr. was no longer the presiding bishop of the Alabama-West Florida Conference. When Bishop W. Kenneth Goodson, the new presiding bishop received word of the Alabama Supreme Court decision, he issued the following statement:

> We are grateful that the court in this decision has upheld the honored tradition of our church in regards to its property.
>
> I do not feel this is a victory over anyone, but rather a vindication of the wisdom of our fathers, who established our form of church government.
>
> My primary concern at this time is for those people in Union Springs who have undergone the tension of this legal conflict. My hope and prayer is for a healing of the divisions through the reconciling love of Christ.
>
> United Methodist property in Union Springs will continue its long tradition as a place for the fellowship and nurture of the

---

[33]T. Leo Brannon, *The Methodist Christian Advocate*, 9 September, 1969. Reverend Brannon served as assistant to W. Kenneth Goodson, resident bishop of the Alabama-West Florida Conference in 1969.

children of God and the faithful proclamation of the gospel of our Lord Jesus Christ.[34]

---

[34]Ibid.

7

ALABAMA CATCHES
ITS BREATH: 1964

... no action is more contrary to the spirit of our democracy and
Constitution—or more rightfully resented by a Negro citizen who
seeks only equal treatment—than the barring of that citizen from
restaurants, hotels, theaters, recreational areas and other public
accommodations and facilities.

—John F. Kennedy, Omnibus Civil Rights Act of 1963

AS THE RACIALLY TROUBLED AND VIOLENT YEAR OF 1963 NEARED ITS
end, Auburn University was ordered to accept its first black student.
Harold A. Franklin, a black, had received a degree in history from the
all-black Alabama State College in May 1962. He had then applied to
the graduate school of Auburn University. Denied admission, Franklin
brought suit in August 1963, charging he was denied admission
because of his race. On November 5, 1963, federal judge Frank M.
Johnson ordered Auburn University to admit Franklin for the next
term scheduled to begin January 2, 1964.[1]

The news of Johnson's decision was greeted in Auburn with
apprehension and heightened tension. The leaders of Auburn knew
that violence and disregard for federal court orders had required the
use of federal troops and federal marshals in Alabama three times in
the past two and a half years.[2] They also remembered the violent crisis
that occurred in Oxford, Mississippi, when James Meredith was

---

[1] *Montgomery Advertiser*, 6 November, 1963

[2] Federal marshals were sent to Montgomery in 1961 to protect the freedom
riders following a day of violence. Federal troops were sent to Birmingham in 1963
after a day of rioting; and the Alabama National Guard was federalized to enforce the
court ordered integration of the University of Alabama in June 1963 when Governor
Wallace blocked the schoolhouse door.

enrolled in September 1962. Similarly, only months earlier Governor Wallace had "stood in the schoolhouse door" of the University of Alabama to block the court ordered admission of Vivian Malone and James Hood. Likewise, it was only a few months since Wallace had sent his troopers into Auburn's neighboring town of Tuskegee to block blacks from entering Tuskegee High School.

Two Methodist ministers in Auburn decided that they should offer assistance in the hope of avoiding a crisis when Franklin came to Auburn in January 1964. Powers McLeod was in his sixth year as the minister of Auburn First Methodist Church and Reverend Maxwell Hale was in his fourth year as the director of the Wesley Foundation, the Methodist ministry to students at Auburn University.

After discreet discussions with key officials at Auburn University, it was decided that Hale would travel quietly to Oxford, Mississippi and consult with friends and contacts he had there at the University of Mississippi. Hale sought advice from these friends on what could be learned from their experiences with Meredith's admission a year earlier.

McLeod had a close personal friend who was a clerk of Supreme Court Justice Hugo Black. Through this friend, he arranged a meeting in Washington, DC with Burke Marshall, head of the Civil Rights Division of the US Justice Department. As a result of these two meetings, McLeod and Hale received valuable information which they were able to share with other concerned community leaders. They also offered their assistance, when and if needed.[3]

The first call for McLeod's assistance came when John Doar and John Douglas of the US Justice Department arrived in Auburn and sought housing accommodations. They discovered that the Alabama State Troopers had taken all the available rooms in the small town of Auburn and the surrounding area. McLeod took Doar as a guest in his home and arranged for Douglas to be the guest of the Presbyterian minister, John Evans.

When Franklin was scheduled on Saturday morning to register and become the first black student at Auburn University, the *Montgomery Advertiser* carried a front page article which read: "Gov. George C.

---

[3] Reverend Maxwell Hale, interview, 27, 28 July, 1994; Reverend Powers McLeod, written interview, 18 June, 1993.

Wallace Friday ordered Col. Al Lingo and his helmeted state troopers to use force if necessary to keep federal agents off Auburn University campus Saturday when Negro Harold A. Franklin is scheduled to enroll." [4]

This development meant that the Justice Department and the FBI had no campus location to set up a command and control center for the protection of Franklin, and an appropriate non-federal escort to assure the safety of Franklin was now a primary, critical issue. McLeod offered his office at the Auburn Methodist Church for use as a command center. McLeod described the events on the critical day of January 4 this way:

> Mr. Doar and I went to my office, which was to become the control center for the Justice Department people . . . In the church parking lot was the Justice Department's communication car. Mr. Douglas could talk to anyone in the country from that car.
>
> Next, Mr. Douglas and John Doar went down to the highway where the new student and Mr. Gray (Mr. Franklin's attorney) were to come into Auburn. The routes they were to use had been agreed on with the state troopers, and everyone knew that the roads would be carefully watched for unauthorized persons . . . "[5]

Around mid-morning, as the time for Franklin's arrival neared, an FBI agent came to the command center to quickly check the campus map. The original plan called for Franklin and his attorney to meet at carefully-placed barriers just off campus to avoid a confrontation with the Alabama state troopers. But as the FBI agent studied the map, it became clear that the barriers had been deliberately moved to a spot several hundred yards inside the campus where a heavily-wooded area could provide concealment for people other than the troopers. A trap had been set. We feared that upon arrival at the barriers, Gray would be arrested by the state troopers and in the confusion a gun or knife could be placed in Franklin's luggage. A similar tactic had been used against James Meredith in his room at the University of Mississippi.

---

[4]*Montgomery Advertiser*, 4 January, 1964.
[5]Reverend Powers McLeod, written interview, 18 June, 1993; Reverend Maxwell Hale, interview 27, 28 July, 1994.

Douglas instructed the agent to bring Franklin to the command center where two FBI agents could search Franklin's luggage before he entered the campus. "That way no one can accuse him of having a concealed weapon."[6]

Thus, thanks in part to the information that Hale had obtained from his visit to the University of Mississippi, as well as the courage of both Hale and McLeod, Franklin and his attorney were brought to McLeod's office for his safety before going to the Auburn campus. As a final precaution, Douglas asked McLeod and his friend Jim Woodson, who was the Episcopal rector in Auburn, to drive behind the car that took Franklin to the campus for registration. Franklin was enrolled without incident and housed in Magnolia Hall.

The Justice Department officials were grateful enough for the assistance received from McLeod that they relayed these events to Attorney General Robert Kennedy. The Attorney General sent a letter of appreciation (see next page for copy of the letter dated January 9, 1964).

Shortly after the episode in Auburn ended in early 1964, the long, eventful months of crisis, that included the Birmingham demonstrations, the University of Alabama integration drama, the closing of Tuskegee High School, and the bombing and deaths at Birmingham's Sixteenth Street Baptist Church, came to a temporary lull. A decade of violence and death that had been center stage in Alabama was now shifting to Mississippi. The tragedy of those years was not over, but Alabama experienced a few months without a racial crisis. For much of 1964, the manpower, resources, and energy of the Civil Rights Movement focused on Mississippi.

In the late fall of 1963, the Council of Federated Organizations was formed (a composite of SNCC, CORE, NAACP, and SCLC), and a plan was put together to have thousands of summer volunteers conduct a Freedom Summer in Mississippi.[7] The National Council of

---

[6]Ibid.

[7]For a detailed review of the plans and activities of Freedom Summer, see: Len Holt, *The Summer That Didn't End* (New York: William Morrow and Co., 1965) and Sally Belfrage, *Freedom Summer* (New York: Viking Press, 1965); and Howard Zinn, *SNCC, The New Abolitionists* (Boston: Beacon Press, 1965), 62-123.

Office of the Attorney General
Washington, D.C.

JAN 9 1964

Reverend Powers McLeod
Auburn Methodist Church
Post Office Box 1290
Auburn, Alabama

Dear Reverend McLeod:

I have been informed by a number of people
how extremely helpful you have been during the past
few weeks in connection with the integration of
Auburn University, as well as in connection with other
matters in the past. There is nothing that we can do
that makes as much difference as what someone like your-
self does within the community where this kind of
problem takes place. I am sure that you realize that
your work has been of benefit not only to Auburn but
to the State of Alabama, regardless of what the Governor
and other political figures there may think now, and
to the country.

Very truly yours,

Attorney General

Churches agreed to donate $50,000 to the project and also provide a site for the basic training of the volunteers.

Freedom Summer began with the brutal murders of James Chaney, Mickey Schwerner, and Andy Goodman in Philadelphia, Mississippi in June. The national shock to this horror both focused the media's attention on Mississippi and also increased the determination of the volunteers pouring into that state to staff the Freedom Summer's freedom schools, community centers, and voter registration projects.[8]

With national attention now on Mississippi, Alabama caught its breath during much of 1964. That is not to suggest that all was quiet. During the year there were racial episodes in Tuscaloosa, Huntsville, Talladega, as well as other locations. But the tone, intensity, and focus were diminished from what it had been in 1963 and earlier years.

THE GENERAL CONFERENCE OF THE METHODIST CHURCH

As the plans for the Freedom Summer project were being finalized, and Alabama was experiencing a welcomed pause from its series of racial crises, the Methodists of the world met in Pittsburgh, Pennsylvania, for their quadrennial meeting of the General Conference. When this conference of representatives of the 11.1 million members of the Methodist Church[9] held its last gathering in 1960, the student sit-in movement was just beginning. In the intervening years the Freedom Rides, the Birmingham demonstrations, the Washington March, and many tragic acts of violence and death had transpired.

It was both natural and inevitable that the dominant theme of the two week conference was centered on this most urgent social crisis confronting America. The conference opened with a central emphasis on civil rights and it closed with a new effort to end segregation within the Methodist Church by eliminating the Central Jurisdiction.[10]

The tone and theme were set on opening day with the presentation of the Episcopal address. After a word of greeting and a memoriam to

---

[8]Holt, *Summer That Didn't End*, 37, 18-30.
[9]*Journal of the 1964 General Conference of The Methodist Church* (Nashville: Methodist Publishing House, 1964), 196.
[10]Ibid., 212-854

the bishops who had died since the last General Conference, the
address continued with these explanatory words:

> The Episcopal Address, while written by one man, is the united word
> of the Council of Bishops to The Methodist Church. It is not our
> purpose to define all contemporary issues, promote all the worthy
> causes, or list specific programs for action in the address. We believe
> the Church expects us to share our hopes and our judgments, and to
> speak out of our love for The Methodist Church . . .

The Episcopal address then covered the ministry of the church, the
growth of the church, the mission of the church, the role of the laity
in the church, and the vision of the church for tomorrow. But the
poignant heart of the Episcopal address was the clear statement on
race covered in a section headed, "Integration." The full text of this
section read:

> The official pronouncements of The Methodist Church on the
> race question are clear. That any minister or layman in The Method-
> ist Church should have any question as to where we stand on this
> issue, is inconceivable. It is, therefore, most disturbing to see
> Methodists trying to justify segregation on the basis of weird
> interpretations of the Scriptures. We are dedicated to the proposi-
> tion that all men are created equal, all men are brothers, and all men
> are of eternal worth in the eyes of God. Prejudice against any person
> because of color or social status is a sin.
>
> Every minister proclaiming this fundamental Christian doctrine
> must have the backing of the whole Methodist Church. Every bishop
> and every district superintendent is bound by the discipline of the
> Church to oppose segregation and discrimination. Compromises in
> this field have brought nothing but shame to us and today we stand
> under the judgment of God. The Church which does not cleanse
> itself of this sickness, brings comfort to the enemies of Christ and
> betrays its Lord.
>
> We believe that this General Conference should insist upon the
> removal from its structure of any mark of racial segregation and we
> should do it without wasting time. This will cost the Negro Method-
> ists some of their minority rights. It will cost some white Methodists
> the pain of rooting out deep-seated and long-held convictions
> concerning racial relations. But God Almighty is moving toward a

world of interracial brotherhood so speedily and so irresistibly, that to hesitate is to fight against God and be crushed.

We believe that this General Conference should be able to say when it adjourns: The people called Methodists, by the grace of God, have moved forward toward removing segregation.[11]

Despite the Episcopal address, the delegates to this 1964 General Conference debated and struggled throughout the conference with the process and time-table of removing the structures of segregation from the Methodist Church. After six days of debate, which at times was heated, and much parliamentary wrangling, the conference delegates finally voted to eliminate the racially segregated Central Jurisdiction within the next four years.[12]

Additionally, the conference passed an important but controversial resolution which supported the principle and practice of civil disobedience. The resolution read:

There are certain circumstances when arbitrary authority is sought to be imposed under laws which are neither just nor valid as law. Even under such imposition the salutary principle of the rule of law requires that in all but the most extreme circumstances the individual confronting such authority must resort to legal processes for the redress of his grievances. However, Christians have long recognized that after exhausting every reasonable legal means for redress of grievances, the individual is faced with the moral and legal dilemma of whether or not his peculiar circumstances require obedience to 'God rather than men.' There are instances in the current struggle for racial justice when responsible Christians cannot avoid such a decision. Wherever legal recourse for the redress of grievances exists, the responsible Christian will obtain the best available legal and religious counsel for his dilemma. In rare instances, where legal recourse is unavailable or inadequate for redress of grievances from laws or their application that, on their face are unjust or immoral, the Christian conscience will obey God rather than man.[13]

---

[11]Ibid., 204-205.
[12]Ibid., 279-365.
[13]Ibid., 1272.

This resolution on civil disobedience was in sharp contrast to the position taken in the statement to King by the eight prominent church leaders during the Birmingham demonstrations in 1963. The General Conference resolution also became a matter of immediate concern to many of the Methodists in the Alabama-West Florida Conference. Between the end of the General Conference on May 8 and the beginning of the Alabama-West Florida Annual Conference on May 26, the Committee on Memorials of the Alabama-West Florida Conference received 124 memorials (petitions). Approximately half of these memorials concerned the "civil disobedience" resolution and the other half ". . . dealt with the National Council of Churches."[14]

THE REACTION OF ALABAMA METHODISTS

When the Methodists of the Alabama-West Florida Conference met at Huntingdon College for their annual conference, an overwhelming majority passed a resolution which rejected the "civil disobedience" resolution passed by the General Conference. Alabama's resolution read:

> We the members of the Alabama-West Florida Conference of The Methodist Church, representing the 130,000 Methodists of our conference wish to record our judgment that The Methodist Church should not lend its support and/or endorsement to any form or degree of civil disobedience."[15]

The Alabama-West Florida Conference then moved immediately to the subject of the National Council of Churches. During this period when sit-ins, kneel-ins, and other forms of demonstrations were occurring, the National Council of Churches' involvement with and support of the Civil Rights Movement had caused a number of local Methodist churches to withhold their financial support. The action of the National Council in supporting Mississippi's Freedom Summer brought the issue to a divisive point, and funding from local churches

---

[14]*Journal of the Alabama-West Florida Conference, The Methodist Church*, 1964, 128.

[15]Ibid., 125

dropped dramatically.[16] In response to this drop in funding and the many memorials received concerning the National Council of Churches, the annual conference passed a resolution requesting the bishop to appoint a committee of five ministers and five laymen to conduct a thorough study of the National Council of Churches and present a report with recommendations to the next annual conference.[17]

Thus, the Methodists of Alabama stated emphatically and clearly that they would in no way march to the tune of the national Methodist Church as expressed by the General Conference. Neither would they agree with or support the actions and pronouncements for racial inclusiveness of the National Council of Churches. The Methodists of Alabama, like all of the other Protestant churches of the state, continued to be totally segregated institutions, and all too often, bastions of resistance.

More Ministerial Departures

The 1964 session of the Alabama-West Florida Annual Conference marked the conclusion of Bishop Hardin's tenure as presiding bishop. A new bishop was scheduled to be elected and assigned to the Alabama area at the Jurisdictional Conference in July 1964.

The three and a half years that Hardin had presided as the temporary bishop of the Alabama-West Florida Conference had been troubled and difficult years. The pressures experienced by most of the ministers during those years had exacted a heavy personal toll. During just those three and a half years, thirty-two ministers of the Alabama-West Florida Conference had either transferred out of Alabama to some other, less troubled area of the country, or simply left the ministry altogether.[18]

At the 1964 Annual Conference when the required Disciplinary question 37 was asked, "Who have been transferred out?", five more names were added to that continuing list of departing ministers.

---

[16]Ibid., Statistical Table No. 2, Part 1, 332.
[17]Ibid., 128.
[18]Ibid., 1961, 97-98; 1962, 88-91; 1963, 109; 1964, 74, 87.

Bishop Hardin addressed the conference on this troubling matter and said:

> I make this announcement with a heavy heart. When I was assigned to the presidency of this Annual Conference I found that for several years the Conference had been losing a number of seminary graduates. For the past three and a half years I have been doing my best to stop this exodus. But, brethren, and now I speak to the laymen, the Bishop can't do it by himself. If these able and well trained men are to be kept in the Alabama-West Florida Conference they must be given the privilege of a free pulpit.
>
> For us to nod approval of a sermon that tells how Jesus broke squarely across the lines of convention and custom, of how Jesus spoke courageously the things that people didn't want to hear—and then to deny the minister called of God the right to speak freely the truth as he understands it seems to me the height of intellectual and spiritual inconsistency. It is not obligatory that laymen agree with a minister, but if the Church is to remain a vital force for good in the community it is necessary that the freedom of the pulpit be protected and preserved."[19]

As I listened to this statement of concern about the attrition among my colleagues and the fervent call for a free pulpit, I was struck with ambivalent feelings. I was grateful for this parting statement as Hardin's tenure as presiding officer of the Alabama-West Florida Conference came to an end. But I was also saddened by the fact that his three and a half years of leadership had not measured up to this plea. He had not only condemned King and the Birmingham protesters in their struggle for equality in public accommodations, but he had used his office as bishop to promote and reward those who had been defenders of the status quo.

During Hardin's tenure he had appointed a total of eight district superintendents to his Cabinet, but only two of those eight were men whose ministry had been committed to an open, just, and racially-inclusive church and society. Likewise, of all the ministers appointed by Bishop Hardin to major churches, only one out of four were filled by ministers who had openly supported the black movement for

---

[19]Ibid., 1964, 74.

equality and justice.[20] The deeds spoke louder than the words. Each year witnessed a continuous exodus of talented young ministers. Each minister had reached his own personal decision of painful separation.

NEW BISHOP, NEW HOPE

In July 1964, the Southeastern Jurisdictional Conference met for its quadrennial meeting at Lake Junaluska, North Carolina. One of the major responsibilities of the conference was to elect new bishops to replace those who had retired or died. W. Kenneth Goodson, a minister of the Western North Carolina Conference, was elected bishop and assigned to the Birmingham Area, which included both the North Alabama Conference and the Alabama-West Florida Conference.

W. Kenneth Goodson was born in Salisbury, North Carolina in 1912. Educated in Salisbury, he graduated from Boyden High School in 1930 during the Great Depression and entered Catawba College in Salisbury. After completing his undergraduate degree in 1934, he attended Duke Divinity School in Durham, North Carolina, graduating with his divinity degree in 1937. Then in October, 1937 he was ordained a deacon in the Methodist Church and joined the Western North Carolina Conference. Two years later he was ordained elder and admitted into full connection in the Western North Carolina Conference where he served a number of pastorates before being elected Bishop in July, 1964 at the age of 51.

Shortly after his election and assignment to Alabama, Bishop Goodson moved into his episcopal residence in Birmingham and, as a first order of business, called a special session of the Alabama-West Florida Conference. The ministers knew little about their new leader but they listened eagerly and expectantly at that first meeting. Nothing profound occurred and little that was memorable was said, but something about this man struck an intuitive chord of hope.

During the coming months and years we would all witness some moments of disappointment, but much more importantly, we discovered that our new bishop represented the Methodist Church's commitment to end segregation in church and society and to provide

---

[20]Ibid., 1961, 104-115; 1962, 104-114; 1963, 114-123; 1964, 90-98.

personal leadership to this end. In the appointment of his ministers, in the selection of his district superintendents, and, perhaps, most important of all, in his personal support of those ministers amid racially-centered crises in their local churches, this bishop demonstrated that he rejected the status quo and believed in and was committed to an open and just society both for today and tomorrow.

Only a few months after his arrival, Bishop Goodson quietly and secretly sent McLeod, Prestwood, and me on a mission to Atlanta to talk with leaders of the Southern Christian Leadership Conference for the purpose of opening a line of communication between the bishop as representative of the Methodist Church in Alabama and the leadership of the SCLC. McLeod at this time was the district superintendent of the Mobile District and one of the nine members of the bishop's cabinet. In this official position, the three of us met with officials of SCLC. Nothing radical occurred at this meeting, but an openness and new spirit of concern and compassion was officially started. Bishop Goodson ushered in a new hope that the church, and particularly the Methodist Church, could help make a difference.

8

VIOLENCE AND DEATH
RETURN TO ALABAMA: 1965

The destruction and the bitterness of racial disorder, the harsh polemics of black revolt and white repression have been seen and heard . . . It is time now to end the destruction and violence, not only in the streets . . . but in the lives of people.

—National Advisory Commission on Civil Disorders

ON 2 JANUARY 1965, JUST SIX MONTHS AFTER CONGRESS HAD PASSED the sweeping 1964 Civil Right Act, Martin Luther King Jr. opened a bold, new campaign to obtain the right to vote. Speaking to hundreds of blacks at Brown Chapel AME Church in Selma, King said, "Today marks the beginning of a determined, organized, mobilized campaign to get the right to vote everywhere in Alabama."[1]

The focus of the voter registration campaign was centered in the town of Selma with simultaneous efforts in surrounding communities including Marion, Greensboro, and Camden. The initial phase of this registration effort involved large numbers of blacks in each of these targeted communities simply walking to the county court house and attempting to register.

This organized effort at registration was resisted at every turn. Local police stopped and sought to disperse the marchers and registration candidates. The Boards of Registrars delayed and obstructed the orderly process of registration. But as the campaign continued day after day, this early resistance turned first to anger and then to violence.

---

[1]*Montgomery Advertiser*, 3 January, 1965.

METHODIST MINISTERS CAUGHT IN THE STORM

Forty miles southwest of Selma, in the small town of Camden, the county seat of Wilcox county, the voter registration effort faced a unique and monumental challenge. Not a single black was registered to vote in Wilcox county even though blacks represented 78 percent of the population. The white community reacted with total resistance to the daily demonstrations and efforts to register.

The minister of the Methodist Church of Camden, Ed Henne, had never been an activist or even an advocate for racial justice. Neither, however, had he been a defender of the status quo. He had, like many, simply remained uninvolved with racial matters both in the church and in the community. With passions running at a fever pitch, however, Henne soon found that he could not remain uninvolved, nor could he keep the community anger out of the church.

The officials of the Camden Methodist Church carried their community anger at the black protests to the church by voting to cease paying all World Service and Conference Benevolence as well as all other "apportionments" that went beyond the local community. Next, the church officials assigned men to stand guard at the church doors each Sunday to make certain that no black could enter. Finally, they sent a formal delegation to Union Springs, Alabama, to visit with leaders of the church that had withdrawn from the Methodist Church. Their mission was to learn what was necessary to withdraw and form an independent church.[2]

While all this was taking place, Henne also encountered the community anger in a more personal way. The Methodist parsonage was located next door to a downtown hotel and his young pre-school son frequently played with the hotel owner's son. According to Henne, during this period of daily demonstrations, ". . . an out-of-state minister who was a field worker with the registration campaign, was badly beaten in the hotel." Traumatically, Henne's young son witnessed this brutal physical assault.[3]

---

[2] Reverend Ed Henne, written interview, 14 July, 1993. Henne was a member of the Alabama-West Florida Conference from 1954 until his retirement in 1992, and was minister at Camden from June 1962 until June 1965.
[3] Ibid.

An hour north of Camden and forty-five miles west of Selma is the small town of Greensboro, the county seat of Hale county. The Methodist Church and parsonage of Greensboro are located on Main Street in downtown, precisely where the protests, marches, and rallies were taking place. The Methodist minister, Ralph Hendricks, described those months of racial activity this way:

> I remember vividly the assembly of a large number of Negroes in the street in front of the parsonage. Their intent was to march to the site of a Negro church that had been destroyed by fire. Implications were that the burning had been deliberate. The local police asked them to disperse and go home or face being tear-gassed. They refused. When the police released the tear-gas, some of it came into the parsonage. Although my family got the effects of the gas, we did not suffer too greatly from it, but it is a memory long etched in our minds.[4]

With this heightened tension and racial crisis a part of Greensboro's daily life, Hendricks felt it was important to re-emphasize his commitment to a church that was open to all people. The next Sunday during the morning worship service Hendricks informed his congregation that they did not have ". . . the right to turn anyone away from Holy Communion who chose to come, anymore than any of us have a right to turn anyone away from the Lord's house of worship."

The reaction to Hendricks' statement was immediate. The very next day five members of his congregation drove to Birmingham to see Bishop Goodson and protest the position of their minister. Hendricks never learned what the five members said to the bishop, but soon discovered, however, that Bishop Goodson had arranged his schedule so that he could come to Greensboro and speak with all the members.

Hendricks describes the visit of Bishop Goodson by saying, "The statement that [Bishop Goodson] made from the pulpit that Sunday was much stronger than the one that I had made." Hendricks then added, "Bishop Goodson was not only my Bishop, but he was a

---

[4]Reverend Ralph Hendricks, written interview, 14 January, 1994. Hendricks was a member of the Alabama-West Florida Conference from 1953 until his retirement in 1988. He was minister at Greensboro from June 1964 until June 1966.

brother to me. He stayed in touch with me by phone two and three times each week during this crisis in Greensboro.[5]

This experience of strong, caring support from Bishop Goodson was new for the ministers of Alabama who faced racial difficulties in their churches. In 1963, while serving a church in racial crisis, I contacted Bishop Hardin only to receive a two-sentence letter stating that he would be out of town for a few days and would contact me upon his return. No further contact was forthcoming.

Another targeted community in the 1965 drive for voting rights was Marion, the county seat of Perry county. Located only thirty miles from Selma, Marion experienced more demonstrations resulting in more arrests and more violence than either Camden or Greensboro. It was at Marion that an outbreak of police violence by Alabama State Troopers resulted in the shooting death of Jimmie Lee Jackson, one of the black demonstrators.[6] For weeks the SCLC had been leading a voter registration drive in Marion. Demonstrations and arrests had led to a protest march by 400 blacks from the Zion Methodist Church to the city jail. Fifty state troopers met the marchers and ordered them to disperse. When the protesters kept marching the troopers charged, wielding billy clubs. In the wild scene that followed many protesters were beaten, several newsmen had their cameras smashed, more than a dozen blacks received injuries requiring medical attention, and a state trooper pulled his revolver and shot 26 year old Jimmie Lee Jackson. Eight days later he died from his wounds.[7]

In the weeks and months of this community anger and violence, Joe Neal Blair encountered great difficulty as minister of the First Methodist Church of Marion. Racial anger was no stranger to Blair. As has been noted earlier, Blair had attended the black rally during the Montgomery bus boycott and had the police report his attendance to his church members. Blair also helped organize, along with J. B. Nichols, an interracial group in Pensacola that accomplished some

---

[5]Ibid.

[6]*Montgomery Advertiser*, 20 February, 1965, 27 February, 1965; Charles E. Fager, *Selma 1965* (New York: Charles Scribner's Sons, 1974), 73-74; Howell Raines, *My Soul Is Rested* (New York: G. P. Putnam's Sons, 1977), 188-189.

[7]*Montgomery Adviser*, February 20, February 27, 1965; Howell Raines, *My Soul Is Rested*, 188-189.

racial progress in that community. Because of these efforts and his involvement, threats were made against him as well as against his school-age children.

His experiences during the Marion turmoil, however, were much more troubling and difficult. The official board of his church had the locks on the doors of the church changed without informing Blair. He was not given a key and could not even get into the church where he was the minister. The officials would unlock the doors and let him in right before the Sunday service began. The officials took turns guarding the doors during the worship services to make certain no blacks could enter. In addition, Blair became the subject of many rumors and criticisms. A false rumor persisted that a northern white minister and his black girlfriend had visited Blair in his office. Then, after NBC newsman Richard Valeriani was injured and hospitalized in the violence the day Jimmie Lee Jackson was shot, Blair was severely criticized for visiting Valeriani in the hospital. Blair's home was constantly watched to keep track of his visitors and activities. Furthermore, the pastoral relations committee of his church "asked him not to use the word 'love' or 'brotherhood'" in the pulpit. Blair refused to comply and was subjected to continuous harassment and criticism because he "let his congregation down and was not on their side."[8]

Blair's most difficult and trying experience during these months of racial strife involved his wife and children. His daughters were told at school that their daddy was a "nigger lover." In addition, many of their playmates would not have anything to do with them. When Blair wife and mother-in-law would go shopping, many of their community neighbors would not even speak to them. But then Blair says, ". . . The brightest spot came when Bishop Goodson heard of our troubles and drove from Birmingham to spend the day with us. He visited us in our home. He even cried with us! Then he walked the streets of Marion with me."[9] After years of little or no support from bishops or conference leaders, Bishop Goodson's genuine, direct support renewed and strengthened those ministers under severe public

---

[8]Reverend Joe Neal Blair, written interview, 13 June, 1993. Blair was minister at Marion First Methodist Church from June 1962 until June 1965.
[9]Ibid.

pressure for their civil rights views. No longer would courageous men have to stand alone.

NATION'S CLERGY INVITED TO SELMA

While these ancillary voter registration campaigns were waged in the Black Belt communities surrounding Selma, the major thrust of King's crusade for voting rights focused on Selma. For months the protests had led to daily arrests with occasional outbreaks of violence, but without any progress in getting blacks registered to vote in Dallas County. Then King announced that they were going to march to the state capitol in Montgomery to present their demands to Governor George Wallace.

On the very Sunday that the march was scheduled to begin, Bishop Goodson arranged his schedule to preach at Church Street Methodist Church in Selma. The bishop had watched the crisis in Selma and the surrounding communities escalate into hardened, angry positions of intransigence, and he wanted to alleviate the mounting tensions.

According to Reverend Warren Lindsey, the district superintendent of the Selma District, Bishop Goodson called and asked him to arrange for his visit to Church Street Methodist Church. This task was not easy for the bishop. The minister of Church Street Methodist Church, George Kerlin, had been an active supporter of the Methodist Layman's Union and a strong defender of maintaining segregation in the church and in society.

Only a few weeks earlier, Kerlin had participated in and supported a decision by the church official board to stop using any Methodist literature as a protest against the literature's support of integration.[10] The bishop hoped that he could help calm the passions while supporting the goal of voting rights for all blacks. At the very hour Bishop Goodson was preaching a message of reconciliation to the Methodists

---

[10]Based on author's personal knowledge and on Reverend Arthur Carlton, written interview, 28 March 1994. Carlton was District Superintendent of the Selma District from June 1966 until June 1972.

of Selma, the police were beating the civil rights marchers on the Edmund Pettus Bridge.[11]

Within hours of the police assault at the bridge, King issued a call to the nation's clergy to come to Selma and join him in a March From Selma To Montgomery and more than 400 Protestant ministers, Catholic priests, and Jewish rabbis responded.[12] The arrival of this clergy invasion was greeted with mixed feelings by the Methodist ministers of Alabama. Obviously, those local ministers who had defended the status quo or chosen to stay uninvolved, resented this intrusion of "outsiders". But more importantly, most of those local ministers who had been engaged and supportive of black aspirations were, at best, ambivalent about these "weekend" activists.

Discussions between the local clergy and visiting clergy indicated tension between the two groups. From the local perspective, these visitors had little, if any, knowledge, understanding, or appreciation of the costly involvement for racial justice that many of us had been engaged in for years. We felt that they were critical, judgmental, naive, and too quick to paint us all with the brush of guilt for not having solved the problem. From their perspective, they were here simply to give tangible support to the march for black voting rights.

Similar meetings were also taking place in other communities. Arthur Carlton, the minister of the First Methodist Church in Demopolis, described a meeting he had.

> . . . four ministers from the north and California showed up at my office and began to castigate the ministers of the South. We had a most interesting visit. I suppose I surprised them by saying that I would probably be in Selma also if I happened to live in California or somewhere up North.
>
> I told them that I chose to come back to Alabama when I could have gone most anywhere after graduating from Duke in 1944. They began to lose some of their judgmental remarks as we shared some of the burdens under which we worked in the South. They were

---

[11]Reverend Warren Lindsey, written interview, 20 April, 1994. Lindsey was District Superintendent of the Selma District from June 1963 until June 1966.

[12]Fager, *Selma*, 97-98; *Newsweek*, 22 March, 1965, 19-20.

surprised to find that we shared the same kind of feelings and understanding of the Gospel.[13]

BISHOP ISSUES PASTORAL LETTER TO METHODISTS

King's campaign for voting rights reached its climax in the March From Selma to Montgomery. The months of struggle had brought violence and death once again to Alabama's soil. In Marion, Jimmie Lee Jackson had been shot and killed; in Selma, the Reverend James Reeb had been savagely beaten to death; and on an isolated stretch of highway US 80, Viola Liuzzo had been shot and killed on the night that the march ended. Alabama was angry, mean-spirited, and violent.

On April 1, 1965, just one week after the march had ended on the steps of the Alabama state capitol, Bishop Goodson called a special session of the two Alabama Annual Conferences (copy of the invitation on next page). At the same time he issued "A Pastoral Letter To The Methodist Church In Alabama." In the two-page letter Goodson called upon the Methodists of Alabama to begin a period of reconciliation, saying:

> In these days of tragic distress for our state, the Christian Church must reaffirm the Gospel of God's love . . . Without recrimination and with no thought of sitting in judgment upon others, we must confess that we have not loved God . . . nor our neighbor as ourselves.
>
> We call upon our people in Alabama to commit themselves to the task of reconciliation. We who profess the name of Christ, must now become the instruments of healing the wounds which have been chronic in our society and now have become acute. The gravity of the situation is obvious to us all. . . .
>
> We now speak because we must. Therefore, we affirm our conviction that violence and brutality are foreign to the Christian faith. We commit ourselves to the elimination of those injustices that bar any of our people from full participation in all the rights of citizenship.
>
> We support the right to vote, and urge the fair administration of voter requirements for all our people. We call upon people of good

---

[13]Reverend Arthur Carlton, written interview, 28 March, 1994.

will of all races to join us in extending avenues of communication and understanding. We feel that no person should be denied the right of participating fully in all the rights, opportunities, and responsibilities offered by a free society.

We pray that God will guide us as we move forward in a continuing program of reconciliation.

The bishop's plea for reconciliation was greeted with both hope and appreciation by many. But the Methodist Layman's Union remained resistant and determined. In response to Bishop Goodson's "Pastoral Letter", the Layman's Union mailed a draft resolution (see copy of the resolution page 112) to every church in Alabama. The petition requested that it be approved and then mailed to the bishop. The struggle to resist any and every change within the church continued, messages of reconciliation notwithstanding.

THE METHODIST CHURCH
BIRMINGHAM AREA
1801 SIXTH AVENUE NORTH
BIRMINGHAM, ALABAMA

W. KENNETH GOODSON
RESIDENT BISHOP

CONFERENCES:
ALABAMA-WEST FLORIDA
NORTH ALABAMA

April 1, 1965

TO ALL MINISTERS IN THE BIRMINGHAM AREA

My dear co-workers in the ministry of Christ:

These last days have been for all of us most heartbreaking and soul-searching. I cannot tell you how heavy my heart has been. I can say to you that this day, more than ever before in my life, I am determined for God to use me in the struggle for reconciliation among all people. I think in this whole situation there is a word that I want to say to each of you. Therefore, I am calling the ministers of the two Annual Conferences to meet with me next week that I may talk to you.

The ministers of the NORTH ALABAMA CONFERENCE will meet at McCoy Methodist Church, Birmingham, Wednesday morning, April 7, at 10:30 A.M.

The ministers of the ALABAMA-WEST FLORIDA CONFERENCE will meet in the First Methodist Church of Andalusia, Thursday morning, April 8, at 10:30 A.M.

These meetings are for ministers only. I just want to talk out of my heart to my preachers for a little while.

I am enclosing "A Pastoral Letter To The Methodist Church In Alabama." You may use this letter in your services Sunday, if you like.

God needs us, and I hope and pray God can use us to bring peace and reconciling love, as we seek a new relationship with God and with each other.

Sincerely and fraternally,

Kenneth Goodson

WKG-bh

Enc.

"A PETITION"

Date_____

To: Bishop Kenneth H. Goodson,
      Birmingham Area,
      The Methodist Church,
      1801 6th Avenue, North,
      Birmingham, Alabama

Recognizing the seriousness of the racial struggle which now prevails throughout our land and how its influences have spread into areas of our church life, creating differences and growing unrest in our Methodist churches and among Methodist people to the great hurt of the Methodist church.

In sincere loyalty to our church and its doctrines and claiming the time honored right to petition, we respectfully request you, as the Bishop-in-charge of the Birmingham area, consisting of the Alabama – West Florida and the North Alabama Conferences of the Methodist church:

1 – To urge all ministers under your appointment to refrain from giving aid or encouragement to agitations, demonstrations, or to attend any meetings or engage in any propaganda that may encourage disobedience to local, state or federal laws. As expressed in your Western Union Wire of March 20th, 1965 to the Ministers of this Conference.

2 – To protest the methods and program of the National Council of Churches continuing its racial policy in this area.

3 – To use the influence of your great office in urging church publication boards to refrain from using the publications of our church as propaganda media to promote racial views repugnant to our church membership in this area.

4 – To encourage the preservation of our present jurisdictional system which formed the basis of the 1939 union with other Methodist bodies to the end that there be no racial intergration in our local churches and annual conferences.

5 – To discourage those in charge of our Wesley Foundations from using these Methodist Institutions as a means of promoting intergration among our students and youth.

6 – To appoint such ministers to our churches, districts, youth centers, and to other fields of Christian service those who both understand and are sympathetic with the deep convictions of the people they are called to serve.

Signed:_____   Church_____
                 Chairman

              _____   District_____
                 Secretary

Dear Fellow Methodist:

Please present this petition to your official board for their approval and mail to Bishop Goodson.

Sincerely yours,

JAMES S. (JIM) MORGAN
P. O. Box 867
Montgomery, Alabama

9

TOKEN INTEGRATION AND THE METHODIST CHURCH: 1965

There is nothing in history to support the thesis that a dominant class ever yields its position or its privileges in society because its rule has been convicted of injustices.

—Reinhold Niebuhr

THE CIVIL RIGHTS MOVEMENT EFFECTIVELY ENDED ON THE STEPS OF THE Alabama State Capitol with the climax of the March From Selma To Montgomery. Within a few months the US Congress passed the 1965 Voting Rights Bill, opening for the first time the opportunity for all qualified blacks to be registered to vote. With this Voting Rights Bill and the 1964 Civil Rights Act, legal segregation was finally ended. Jim Crow was dead.

The battle then turned to one of implementation. The new laws needed to be tested and proven. Open access had to be established. Openness in motels, restaurants, theaters, and elsewhere, as well as registration to vote, had to be accomplished.

In many communities, business leaders and ministers began working together behind the scenes to help avoid conflict and confrontation as Alabama businesses began complying with the new laws and integrating their facilities. Joel D. McDavid, the minister of First Methodist Church in Montgomery told of such an involvement. As he portrayed it:

> I joined with the YMCA Secretary and a black minister in promoting and helping put together a bi-racial committee for the city. Some of the leading business people shared in this project. Winton "Red" Blount served as the chairperson of the committee and I served as chair of the Public Services Subcommittee.

Our Subcommittee held meetings of hotel and motel owners as well as restaurant proprietors. We worked with them in their concern about economic losses that might occur because of integration. We urged them to abide by the law and did everything we could to give them encouragement as they integrated their facilities.[1]

McDavid also told of experiencing the first token integration of his church worship services. An organized kneel-in at First Methodist Church occurred in the weeks immediately after the Selma March. On two consecutive Sundays, ". . . ten blacks came with two whites to attend the morning worship service. They were welcomed and seated," according to McDavid. He then went on to say, ". . . Our service was televised and they were seen on television. You may know that all did not agree and it was time for me to face the difficulty of trying to be pastor of a congregation who were not all in one accord."[2]

Many other Methodist ministers were also leaders and participants in the peaceful transition to an integrated society. I was actively involved in such a role with business and civic leaders in Tallassee, where I was minister of the First Methodist Church. I was also aware of similar efforts by several other Methodist ministers in their communities.

In addition, I taught a course for black ministers at Tuskegee Institute, sponsored by the National Council Of Churches and funded by a Ford Foundation Grant. The course provided instructions and workshops on voter registration. As leaders in the black communities, these ministers were especially key to a full, effective implementation of their newly won legal rights. The course was centered on assisting them in this role.[3]

----

[1]Bishop Joel D. McDavid, written interview, 27 April, 1994. McDavid was an active member of the Alabama-West Florida Conference from 1944 and was elected as a bishop of the Methodist Church in 1972. McDavid retired in 1984.

[2]Ibid.

[3]Robert Smith, a black Methodist minister, was director of Religious Extension Service for Leadership Education at Tuskegee Institute. This special education program was jointly sponsored by Tuskegee Institute and the National Council of Churches, and funded by a Ford Foundation Grant. One of the courses offered in this special program was the one I taught to black ministers.

The reality of a changed world was beginning to dawn on the citizens of Alabama. Though lacking a willing acceptance of these rapid, radical changes, Alabama seemed resigned to a reality that was becoming the order of the day. In this environment of resignation, many communities turned to ad hoc groups to assist in the transition, and many Methodist ministers willingly involved themselves in these efforts.[4]

Scopes Project and the Summer of 1965

With the focus shifting to implementation, the Southern Christian Leadership Conference structured a plan to concentrate on voter registration for the summer of 1965. The "Summer Community Organization and Political Education" project, commonly referred to as SCOPE, was designed and led by Reverend Hosea Williams of SCLC.[5] The project called for the recruitment of hundreds of college students to come and spend the summer working in the South's Black Belt counties. The student volunteers were to be trained at a workshop on the campus of Morehouse College in Atlanta and then assigned to specific counties to work at registering black voters as well as participating in other civil rights projects.

Charles Prestwood, the Methodist minister of Whitfield Memorial Methodist Church in Montgomery, learned of the SCOPE project through his friends at SCLC and through his contacts on the Alabama Advisory Committee of the US Civil Rights Commission. He was immediately concerned about securing the safety of these students and preventing the kind of violence Mississippi had experienced during the 1964 "Freedom Summer" project.

---

[4]To list all the various community involvement efforts of Methodist ministers during this period would be difficult and lengthy. I have records through my interviews of such involvement by Dr. Charles Prestwood, Reverend Powers McLeod, Reverend Joe Neal Blair, Reverend Ralph Hendricks, Reverend Stanley Mullins, Dr. J. B. Nichols, Reverend Dallas Blanchard, and I am confident that there were many more.

[5]For details of the SCOPE project see: Adam Fairclough, *To Redeem The Soul of America, The Southern Christian Leadership Conference and Martin Luther King Jr.* (Athens: University of Georgia Press, 1987), 258, 262-265, 269; Charles F. Fager, *Selma, 1965* (New York: Charles Scribner's Sons, 1974), 167ff, 201ff.

During the six years since Prestwood returned to Alabama in 1959, he had been one of the most, if not the most, actively engaged Methodist ministers in the civil rights struggle occurring in Alabama.[6] He was personally acquainted with most of the leaders of SCLC and SNCC as well as many local black leaders, and he was respected and trusted by those who knew him. He also had extensive acquaintances within the academic community and within the national leadership of the Methodist Church.

These relationships coupled with his personal commitment and courage were quickly recognized by Bishop W. Kenneth Goodson. The two of them developed a unique working partnership. It was a partnership in which Prestwood tried to take the bishop farther and faster than the bishop felt comfortable in going, but one in which Goodson did what he felt he could do to bring about the goals and aspirations of the Civil Rights Movement.

Shortly after Prestwood learned the details of the SCOPE project, he called Goodson. In their discussion, a plan of assistance emerged and shortly thereafter, I received a call from Prestwood asking me to join him in a trip to Atlanta to meet with Reverend Hosea Williams and attend the last two days of the SCOPE training session at Morehouse College.

This plan of assistance involved our providing a list of names and telephone numbers of individuals in each of the Black Belt counties where the students would be assigned. These individuals were persons who could be called for assistance in any emergency or crisis. Williams, in turn, provided us with the names and location assignments of each of the student volunteers coming into Alabama. We hoped that with such planning and local support, all violence could be avoided and black registration could continue peacefully.

---

[6]The author had the good fortune of being a close, personal friend of Charles Prestwood. Additionally, both of our church pastoral appointments from 1959 through 1968 were located close together. Thus, we worked closely together on many projects, were together on almost a weekly basis, and discussed many topics in substantial detail. This is the basis of my judgment that Prestwood was probably the most actively involved Methodist minister in Alabama during the civil rights movement.

BLACKS IN THE ALABAMA-WEST FLORIDA CONFERENCE

In June of 1965, Joe Lisenby was appointed as the minister of the Pleasant Grove Methodist Church located on the outskirts of Pensacola, Florida. The Pleasant Grove community was primarily a neighborhood of active and retired naval military families and civil service employees at the Pensacola Naval Station. A unique vicinity with many non-Southern residents, Pleasant Grove did not reflect the usual biases of the surrounding communities.

Shortly after Lisenby arrived at Pleasant Grove, a black naval officer and his family moved into the community and were invited to the Pleasant Grove Methodist Church. After they attended services and grew interested in the church, Lisenby invited them to join. Lisenby said of their joining, "It was no big deal. They were in the community . . . they were welcomed . . . it was not a local issue that they were black."[7]

When word reached Bishop Goodson that Lisenby had received a black family as members of the Pleasant Grove Methodist Church, the bishop called to express his support. ". . . [Bishop] Goodson called and congratulated me," according to Lisenby, ". . . on receiving the first black family into the Alabama-West Florida Conference."[8] A small step had been taken, but throughout the Conference the wall of segregation remained.

BLACK AND WHITE METHODIST CONGREGATIONS MERGE

In the late spring of 1965 Reverend Powers McLeod, the District Superintendent of the Mobile District, telephoned Dallas Blanchard, the Methodist minister of the Fort Deposit Methodist Church. He informed Blanchard that Bishop Goodson was searching for a minister willing to be appointed to the Toulminville Methodist Church in Mobile for the purpose of integrating that congregation.

---

[7]Reverend Joe Lisenby, written interview, 8 December, 1993. Lisenby, a member of the Alabama-West Florida Conference who joined the conference in 1962, is still active.

[8]Ibid.

This unusual request originated a series of conversations between McLeod and Goodson concerning the changing demographics of Toulminville and the challenge and opportunity presented by these changes. McLeod had been studying this community and its rapid demographic transition. Blacks were moving in and whites were slowly departing. It seemed clear to McLeod that the Toulminville Methodist Church would soon be in a predominantly black neighborhood, but would have a congregation of white members who lived elsewhere and only drove into Toulminville for church services.

There was also another factor that McLeod included in his discussions with Goodson. Many of the blacks who were moving into the Toulminville community were Methodists who were members of the historic all black Warren Street Methodist Church. Warren Street was a part of the Negro Central Jurisdiction and, thus, a part of a different conference.

The Warren Street Methodist Church was founded in 1889 and was the largest black Methodist church in Alabama and one of the most influential black churches of Mobile. From 1952 until 1961, Joseph Lowery [9] was the minister of Warren Street Methodist Church and under his leadership the church became deeply involved in the civil rights movement. [10]

McLeod's desire to bring these two congregations together during this transitional period was a very bold and positive move, and one Bishop Goodson supported. An official merger of the two congregations was not considered viable since it would require the formal approval of both the Alabama-West Florida Conference and the all-black Central Alabama Conference. However, a functional and less formal union of the two congregations provided a creative way for the Methodist Church to serve the total community.

In his telephone conversation with Blanchard, McLeod covered all the details of the Toulminville situation and then asked Blanchard ".

---

[9]Reverend Joseph Lowery was one of the original organizers of the Southern Christian Leadership Conference in 1957, and is the past the president of the SCLC.

[10]Based on the written history of the Warren Street Methodist Church which is displayed in the Afro-American section of the Mobile City Museum.

. . would he go." In recalling this unusual request, Blanchard said, "I jumped at it and went in June, 1965."[11]

Soon after Blanchard's arrival in Mobile as the newly-appointed minister of the Toulminville Methodist Church, he began to have conversations with the minister of Warren Street Methodist Church. Over a period of months, the two ministers worked on a strategy designed to join together the two congregations into one Methodist Church. Both ministers then began conversations with their respective official boards to engage them in a full discussion of establishing a functionally united church.

The reaction within the Toulminville Methodist Church was immediate and negative. Between June of 1965 when Blanchard arrived and began these conversations, and June 1966, 125 members of the Toulminville Methodist Church transferred their membership to other churches. This exodus represented 23 percent of the total Toulminville membership. [12] In spite of this substantial loss, Blanchard continued to move forward with the plan for a functionally united church.

His next step was to arrange direct discussions between the official board of the Toulminville Methodist Church and the official board of the Warren Street Methodist Church. Blanchard recounted, ". . . we finally invited them [Warren Street members] to join us in a functional united parish since they were moving into our community . . . We held a uniting communion service . . . few of my folks attended, and almost all of them disappeared within three months or so."[13]

Those early months of union were difficult. Not only did 125 parishioners sever their membership the first year of this unique experiment, but between June, 1966, and June, 1967, an additional 246 members transferred their membership to other churches. In just two years the total membership of the Toulminville Methodist Church

---

[11]Dr. Dallas Blanchard, written interview, 9 March, 1994. Blanchard was a minister of the Alabama-West Florida Conference from 1960 to 1968. In 1968, Blanchard returned to his education and completed his doctorate at Boston University. Today Blanchard is head of the Department of Sociology and Anthropology at the University of West Florida.

[12]*Journal of the Alabama-West Florida Conference, The Methodist Church*, 1965, 1966, Statistical Table No 1, Part 1.

[13]Blanchard, interview, 9 March, 1994.

had gone from 557 to only 244. More than half the membership left during the two years of preparation and implementation of the plan of union.[14] Blanchard also said that ". . . some folks wanted to remove the brass commemorative plaques from pews . . . given in memory of their ancestors . . . One family wanted us to return the offering plates given in memory of Mama, but we regretted that we could not give away church property."[15]

In addition to the withdrawal of over half of the members, most of the whites who remained members refused to attend any of the services or participate in any of the church activities. This white resistance to an integrated Methodist Church was not limited to Toulminville alone. Many other Methodist churches in Mobile and elsewhere opposed what was happening at Toulminville. Blanchard set forth the reaction this way:

> We attended Methodist Youth Fellowship sub-district meetings, sent our kids to senior assembly at Huntingdon College, and went to all Methodist events. I never called ahead to warn anyone—we were Methodists and just acted like normal Methodists. Parents came to Huntingdon to take their kids home, churches threatened to withdraw, the Bishop caught hell.[16]

According to Blanchard, Bishop Goodson was under increasing pressure from dissatisfied laymen, ministers and other churches in the conference to close down the Toulminville project since there were very few white members participating. Goodson arranged a meeting of the church trustees to review the situation and make a decision.

After meeting with the two white and three black trustees to discuss both the challenges and opportunities of this project, the bishop took a recess. He walked with Blanchard to the basement of the church. There he observed many youth engaged in activities. Then according to Blanchard, the bishop returned to the meeting and said,

---

[14]*Journal of the Alabama-West Florida Conference,* 1965, 1966, 1967; Statistical Table No 1, Part 1.

[15]Blanchard, interview, 9 March, 1994.

[16]Ibid.

"What you are doing here is just too important to lose. We can't close this church."[17]

The bold attempt to structure a functionally-integrated Methodist Church in Toulminville continued, but the pressures on Blanchard were frightfully difficult. In my number of interviews with him, Blanchard mentioned the following pressures he encountered:

> Some sweet lady would call my wife every time I left home and ask my wife if she knew where our daughter (about four years old) was and if she were safe. We placed our daughter in a bedroom upstairs on the back side of the parsonage, since that appeared to be the safest room in case of a bomb.
>
> We received heavy breathing, silent phone calls every hour on the hour, every day from 11 p.m. to 5 a.m. I called the phone company and they told me to keep a log for a couple of weeks. I told them I didn't need to since they were on the hour from 11 to 5. We kept the log for two weeks, then we got no more calls. I concluded that they were being made by Southern Bell execs on the night shift.
>
> The police were notified that a bomb had been placed in the church. They said they had an informer tell them the Prichard KKK had planted one. None was found.[18]

Three and a half years after Blanchard received the telephone call from McLeod asking him to go to Toulminville and integrate that church, Dallas Blanchard withdrew as minister of the Toulminville Methodist Church and entered graduate school at Boston University. There he earned his doctorate and then entered a new career as a college professor. Blanchard said that when he went to Bishop Goodson to inform him of this decision the bishop ". . . did try to talk me out of it saying that he had wanted to prove that I was appointable to a white pastorate after Toulminville." Blanchard then says, "I responded that I and my family had proved as much as I was willing to for him and declined any further honors."[19]

---

[17]Ibid.
[18]Ibid.
[19]Ibid.

CONTINUED METHODIST RESISTANCE

Token integration had finally come to the Methodist Church in the Alabama-West Florida Conference. The seating of the black and white kneel-in demonstrators at Montgomery's First Methodist Church; the receiving of the first black family as members at Pleasant Grove Methodist Church; and the functionally-integrated congregation at Toulminville Methodist Church were all first steps in the long and difficult struggle to bring the church in line with its teachings and its official pronouncements. But resistance to an integrated, inclusive church continued in most local congregations as well as the formal actions of the Alabama-West Florida Annual Conference.

At the 1965 Annual Conference, a resolution opposing Methodist support of the National Council of Churches was presented and heatedly debated. Additionally, strong opposition was mounted against the report of the Board of Christian Social Concerns which called on each church to provide every Methodist family with a copy of the booklet *The Methodist Church And Race*.

The white Methodists of Alabama were far from ready to accept the changes occurring in the secular society all around them. Instead of leading the rapid changes as might have been expected and hoped for, the church remained an institution rigidly resistant to change.

This resistance even took the form of a physical altercation at the Tuskegee Methodist Church. The occasion was a charge conference at which the district superintendent of the Montgomery District, Wilbur Walton, was the guest minister. For several weeks prior to the charge conference, black students and teachers from Tuskegee Institute had been attempting to attend Sunday worship services. Ushers serving as guards had blocked their entry and prevented them from attending the worship service.

On this particular Sunday morning in 1965, however, the black students came to a back door of the church that was not guarded by ushers. They entered the church and seated themselves for the worship service. After stunned moment of confusion, and in the presence of District Superintendent Walton and A. E. Price, the minister of Tuskegee Methodist Church, the ushers physically picked the black students up and threw them out the church door. Neither Walton or Price objected to or tried to stop the physical confrontation. In fact,

Walton proceeded with the service of worship as if nothing had happened.

At the conclusion of the service, one of the members of the Tuskegee Methodist Church was so incensed by what she had seen that she went to the minister's study to speak with Walton. Francis Rush, a lifelong member of the Tuskegee Methodist Church, confronted Walton about the events she had witnessed. In describing her conversation with Walton, she said, "I asked him how, as a District Superintendent and official representative of The Methodist Church, he could just stand and watch the ushers do what they did and not even have anything to say about it." Walton's only response was, "Well, each church has to tend to its own affairs."[20]

---

[20]Francis Rush, taped interview, October, 1994. Rush was a lifetime member of the Tuskegee First Methodist Church.

10

WHEN WILL THE CHURCH BELL RING? 1966-1976

The work goes on, the cause endures, the hope still lives, and the dream shall never die.

> —Senator Edward Kennedy,
> 1980 speech to the Democratic
> Convention

WITH THE POSSIBLE EXCEPTION OF PRIVATE COUNTRY CLUBS, THE church remained the most segregated institution of the South in 1966. Twelve years after the United States Supreme Court declared segregated schools unconstitutional, two years after the Omnibus 1964 Civil Rights Bill that outlawed segregation in public accommodations, and a year after the Voting Rights Bill opened registration to all blacks of the South, the white church continued to ring its bell only for white parishioners. As Martin Luther King Jr., said at the Methodist Conference in Chicago in 1963, "At 11:00 o'clock on Sunday morning when we sing 'In Christ there is no east or west,' we are in the most totally segregated hour of the week."

In his book *A New Breed Of Clergy*, Charles Prestwood highlighted the hypocrisy of the church's segregation practice by telling of a drawing that was featured in the *Kansas City Call* in the spring of 1959. The drawing depicted a black youth in handcuffs with a tag attached to the handcuffs that listed these grievances:

You can't enter here!
You can't ride here!
You can't play here!
You can't study here!
You can't eat here!
You can't drink here!

> You can't work here!
> You can't worship here!

Prestwood then wrote:

> As a result of the passage of the Civil Rights Acts of 1960, 1964, and
> 1965 . . . and the heroic leadership of some famous and many
> unknown Americans, seven of the eight grievances attached to the
> handcuffs of the young Negro in the drawing can be checked off.
> Places to study, eat, drink, ride, play, enter, and work have long
> since been opened to the Negro by the cumbersome secular forces
> . . . but they still face the strange claim of the churches that they
> can't worship here.[1]

This blatant contradiction between the church's pronouncements
and its practices became the center of protest in the spring of 1966.
Black civil rights activists chose Montgomery, the birthplace of the
civil rights movement, as the prime location to focus their protest
against church segregation. A series of kneel-in demonstrations were
organized and directed at several Methodist churches in Montgomery.
In the weeks immediately preceding Easter Sunday, groups of black
and white worshipers came Sunday after Sunday to seek admission for
worship at each of the targeted Methodist churches. In all cases they
were denied admission and turned away. The story of this refusal by
Methodist churches to admit black worshipers was prominently
featured in local newspapers and on local television.

With the restaurants, motels, theaters, schools, and libraries of
Montgomery openly accepting blacks, it was a humiliating embarrassment to Bishop Kenneth Goodson that Methodist churches in
Montgomery in 1966 were refusing to admit blacks to worship. This
rejection of black worshipers was a direct challenge to Goodson's
leadership and it was in clear violation of the official position of the
Methodist Church. Thus, Goodson was determined to remove this
embarrassment from the church and to find some way to end the
kneel-ins.

---

[1]Charles Prestwood, *The New Breed of Clergy* (Grand Rapids: William B.
Eerdmans, 1972), 82-83.

The bishop was in Pensacola on church business the week prior to Easter and he called Prestwood in Montgomery and asked him to fly to Pensacola to help him find a way to end the Montgomery kneel-ins. Also invited to the meeting were Reverend Powers McLeod, the district superintendent of the Mobile District, Dan Whitsett, the minister of First Methodist Church in Pensacola, and Tom Butts, the minister of the nearby First Methodist Church in Foley, Alabama. All of these men had been long time activists in civil rights matters and they each commanded the respect of the bishop.

The meeting began with the bishop saying to Prestwood that we simply had to do something to "call off the dogs." Even if only temporarily, the Methodist Church needed an end to the kneel-ins. Prestwood's response was quick and pointed, but it was not what Goodson wanted to hear. He said to the bishop, "I don't want to call off the dogs. I wish they would picket every church in Alabama until we stopped hiding from our principles and our responsibilities."[2]

There was a moment of stunned silence and then the other invited guests of the meeting expressed agreement with Prestwood. A long, difficult discussion followed without any solution or plan of action. Then the bishop, in almost a helpless plea asked ". . . but what are we going to do? We must get this crisis of attention off our churches if we are going to work at changing this situation."

Prestwood finally said what the bishop wanted to hear. "Bishop," he said. "I'll make the calls. I'll take care of your problem. But I'm not going to ask them to call off the kneel-ins. I'm going to invite them all to come to my church and bring the newspaper reporters and television cameras with them. We will welcome them."[3]

The bishop had settled his immediate problem. The meeting ended. Upon his return home Prestwood used his many friendships and relationships within the civil rights organizations and Montgomery's black community to fulfill his commitment to Goodson. On Easter Sunday, with the television cameras rolling, Prestwood

---

[2]Charles Prestwood, contemporaneous interview and the notes I made of that discussion; Reverend Powers McLeod, telephone interview, 25 June, 1993.
[3]Ibid.

welcomed a large group of blacks to his service of worship at the Whitfield Memorial Methodist Church.[4]

The reaction of his congregation was immediate and the price he paid was severe. Within the first few weeks after Prestwood welcomed the blacks to his church, the financial support of many of its members had been withdrawn. Two and a half months later at annual conference the members of his church demanded his removal. After only two years as minister at Whitfield Memorial Methodist Church, Goodson reassigned Prestwood to the Warrington Methodist Church in Pensacola, Florida, where the heavy military and non-southern membership of that congregation made the appointment of this controversial minister possible. Only three years later, in 1969, Prestwood, like many of us before and after him, left the pastoral ministry and the Alabama-West Florida Conference. He accepted the position of chairman of the Sociology Department at Albright College in Reading, Pennsylvania. In 1979 while undergoing a second heart transplant, Prestwood died. He had specifically requested that his body be cremated and his ashes scattered over Greene county, Alabama, where he served his first pastoral appointment, over the Edmond Pettus Bridge in Selma, and at the walkway of the First Methodist Church in Brewton, Alabama, where he began his journey. Reverend Tom Butts, one of his friends who remained in the Alabama-West Florida Conference, carried out his wish.[5]

The kneel-ins that so disturbed and embarrassed Bishop Goodson and proved to be so costly to Prestwood were not limited to Montgomery alone. Many other communities were also confronted with the repeated efforts of blacks to come and worship at white Methodist churches.

---

[4]Charles Prestwood, contemporaneous interview; Reverend Tom Butts, written interview, 24 September, 1993; Reverend Powers McLeod, written interview 18 June, 1993. Additionally, the meeting is discussed in a self-published book, Powers McLeod, *Southern Accents, Different Voices* (Pensacola, FL: Ardara House Publishers,, 1993), 84-85.

[5]Charles Prestwood served ten years from 1959 to 1969 in the pastoral ministry of the Alabama-West Florida Conference. He maintained his conference membership in that conference even though he taught sociology at Albright College from 1969 until his death in 1979. In 1972 his book, *A New Breed of Clergy*, was published and he was working on a second book on the church in Alabama at the time of his death.

In locations as scattered as Marion, Jackson, Mobile, Selma, and Tuskegee, blacks came to Methodist churches to worship only to be turned away. Most of these confrontations were not covered by the press and did not receive the attention of the pre-Easter Montgomery kneel-ins. But the kneel-ins around the state continued and highlighted the dilemma and hypocrisy of the church's failure to ring its bell for all God's children.

In Tuskegee two of the women who were involved with the kneel-ins were quite upset by the church's refusal to admit and welcome blacks to its service of worship. On 27 June 1967 they wrote the following letters to the minister, Billy Frank Hall:

Dear Rev. Hall,
     I came as a guest to your church last Sunday with the hope of having a sermon and leadership equal to the challenge of these times. With my white skin and Sunday dress I entered your front doors without incident. Shortly afterward, those doors were locked. I heard a knock on the front doors as a group of Negro and white young people tried in vain to come in. I was struck by the similarity of that incident to the picture of Christ knocking on a door without a latch.
     As I sat through that service, I wondered how much meaning the weekly ritual carried. I had the feeling that Christ met outside those walls with the small group which had their own worship on the front steps. What is a "church" anyway?

Sincerely,
Marlene Ellis

Dear Mr. Hall:
     As someone who has been raised in a [C]hristian home and who is healthily questioning the work of the modern church, I have several questions to ask of you. These questions were prompted after attempting to worship both inside and outside of your building. Also as a teacher of young children I feel somehow I need to find answers that allow me to function as a person living in a changing and closely related world.
     Why are there boundries [*sic*] to the love that Christ proclaimed we must have for everyone? Would Christ have kept anyone from following Him? What is it that separates man from man? What

allows a person to condemn others before he has first done everything to understand and appreciate what that person is and can be?
Shouldn't we be concerned with knowing individuals and not
pigeon-holing them according to some physical feature? How can we
teach children to respect and appreciate all men when the image they
get from adults is one of tearing down and degrading others?

Somehow I feel we need to get our values in prospective [sic]
and look at all men with love. How can we do this when church
doors are locked? Or is the church and its god really dead?

Sincerely,
Margaret Cooper
c/o School of Home Economics
Tuskegee Institute

These two women along with many other blacks had come for a
number of months to the First Methodist Church of Tuskegee to seek
to worship. One of the women was white and was admitted for
worship, but in all cases the blacks were turned away. The blacks
would then kneel and conduct their own service of worship outside
the locked doors of the church. Their singing and praying could be
heard inside the sanctuary where "whites only" were gathering for
worship.[6]

The letters these two women wrote to Hall raise the profound
question of "What is a 'church' anyway?" and ". . . is the church and
its god really dead?" The answer in the case of the Tuskegee Methodist Church and the many other Methodist churches that turned away
God's children because they were black was self-evident and placed a
stain of shame on the Methodist Church.

As these kneel-ins were occurring in Montgomery, Tuskegee,
Marion, Selma, Mobile and elsewhere there were many voices that
questioned the motives and intentions of these activists who came to

---

[6]Francis Rush, taped interview conducted by Glyn Brown, the daughter of Donald
G. Brown, Methodist minister at Tuskegee from 1968 to 1970. Reverend Powers
McLeod, telephone interview, 25 June, 1993. McLeod was District Superintendent
of the Montgomery District and the Methodist minister at Tuskegee Methodist
Church from June 1966 to June 1970. Reverend Don Brown, telephone interview,
May 1995. Note: Brown refused to accept the appointment to Tuskegee until and
unless the policy of refusing to admit blacks for worship was officially rescinded.

test the openness of the church. "Were they really coming to worship?" was a frequent question asked. Another common reaction was, "They are just grandstanding to get attention and are not really interested in harmony and worship." But the real question is not their motives or even their behavior, rather it is the openness of God's church and it's welcome to all God's children, black or white, drunk or sober, rich or poor, saint or sinner. When a church bell rings, its invitation is to all.

First Black Graduates from Formerly All-white High Schools

In the late spring of 1966, several formerly all white high schools were graduating their first black students. It had only been two and a half years earlier, in the fall of 1963, that Alabama had been under court order to admit its first black students to public school below the university level. A few of those black students were in the 1966 graduating class.

One of those black seniors scheduled for graduation was at Wetumpka High School in Elmore County. This student would be the first black ever to graduate from Wetumpka High. The school principal knew that the situation would likely be tense and potentially dangerous and so he prepared early and carefully for this historic first. I was invited to give the graduation address and gladly accepted.

As the date of graduation grew near, the family of the graduating black student received numerous threats as did the school principal. A week or so before graduation day the local bank applied economic pressure to the family to encourage the black youth to withdraw from graduation. Then just a few nights before graduation, the home of this black family was burned to the ground and threats were delivered to the school that no black would live to walk across the stage and receive a diploma.

The FBI was brought into this crisis situation and on graduation night as I arrived to present the graduation address there appeared to be almost as many FBI agents present as there were family members. Bomb threats had been received and the warning that no black would live to walk across the stage had been repeated.

One could almost smell the fear in the school auditorium. Sitting backstage, we still did not know if the FBI would vacate the building or allow the program to proceed. Then a few minutes before the scheduled time to begin, the FBI said we could proceed, but that we should speed through the process as quickly as possible. I told them I would limit my remarks to five minutes, which I did. The principal read the names and presented the diplomas almost as rapidly. No further violence occurred, but the atmosphere of fear and strain can never be forgotten.

PLAN OF UNION: MORE PRESSURE FOR CHANGE

During the summer and fall of 1966 while blacks were systematically being turned away from many Methodist churches in Alabama, a special session of the General Conference of the Methodist Church was being held in Chicago. The purpose of this special session was to formulate and approve a plan of union between the Evangelical United Brethren Church and the Methodist Church to form the United Methodist Church. These two denominations had been engaged in discussions about a plan of union for a number of years and final preparations were underway for a uniting conference to be held in Dallas in April, 1968.

Central to the structure of the plan of union was the elimination of all racial barriers within The United Methodist Church. Under the terms of Division One, Article IV, the plan of union clearly declared:

> The United Methodist Church is a part of the Church Universal which is one body in Christ. Therefore all persons, without regard to race, color, national origin, or economic condition, shall be eligible to attend its worship services, to participate in its programs, and, when they take the appropriate vows, to be admitted into its membership in any local church in any connection. In The United Methodist Church no conference or other organizational unit of the church shall be structured so as to exclude any member or any constituent body of the church because of race, color, national origin, or economic condition."[7]

---

[7]*Journal of the Alabama-West Florida Conference, The Methodist Church*, 1967, 178.

In addition to adopting a constitution that included this article, the 1966 special session of the General Conference included in its Enabling Legislation the following:

> So far as the Annual Conferences formerly of the Methodist Central jurisdiction (all-black) are concerned, efforts shall be made to carry out the "Plan of Action for the Elimination of the Central Jurisdiction" as adopted by the Methodist General Conference of 1964. This Plan of Action outlines and urges a procedure designed to bring about the elimination of the Central Jurisdiction by September 1, 1967. The carrying out of the Plan of Action was entrusted by the General Conference to a quadrennial Commission on Interjurisdictional Relations consisting of twenty-four (24) members, four (4) from each Jurisdiction, the four members in each case constituting a Jurisdictional Commission. The General Conference Commission of twenty-four is specifically charged:
>
> 10. If by September 1, 1967, for any reason, the Central Jurisdiction shall not have been dissolved by the procedure of Amendment IX (47ix), the commission shall draft a plan for its termination to report to the General Conference of 1968.[8]

The Enabling Legislation for the uniting conference in Dallas then said in emphatic terms:

> The 1966 session of the Methodist General Conference unmistakably expressed its determination to bring about not only the elimination of the Central Jurisdiction but also the merger of the separate Negro Annual Conferences formerly part of that Jurisdiction with the conferences of the Regional Jurisdictions and the elimination of any structural organization based on race. The resolution adopted by the General Conference and submitted by it to the other bodies named therein reads in part:
> By the adoption of this resolution each Annual Conference , each Jurisdictional Conference, the General Conference, each College of Bishops, and the Council of Bishops express their determination to do everything possible to bring about the elimina-

---

[8]Ibid., 189.

tion of any structural organization in the Methodist Church based on race at the earliest possible date. . . .[9]

The Methodists of Alabama were scheduled to meet for their annual conference in May 1967. At that conference every delegate would have the responsibility to vote on the Plan of Union, on a Resolution for the Elimination of Racial Structures, and also elect the delegates to the Dallas Uniting Conference. In preparation for this difficult and controversial task, Bishop Goodson appointed a Tri-Conference Advisory Committee to meet, plan for, and make recommendations to the upcoming annual conference concerning these controversial matters.

The advisory committee consisted of officially appointed representatives from the all-white North Alabama Conference, the all-white Alabama-West Florida Conference, and the all-black Central Alabama Conference. They met and organized on April 7, 1967, and elected Reverend Paul Duffey chairman.

Duffey and his fellow-committee members were confronting no small task. The US Congress had managed to pass three major, definitive civil rights laws during the 1960s in spite of the formidable opposition and filibuster skill of southern senators. But the Methodist Church had been unable to move at all on the subject of segregated church structures and practices.

One of the first actions of the committee was to establish an agenda designed to fully inform all Methodists of Alabama on the issues to be decided at the next annual conference. As part of this preparation,

> [t]he committee prepared for the publication of a statement entitled, "The Issues Before Us." This was distributed through the courtesy of the Board of Christian Social Concerns of the Alabama-West Florida Conference for the purpose of informing all of our people of matters relating to the elimination of the Central Jurisdiction.[10]

---

[9]Ibid.
[10]Ibid., 194.

In addition the committee carefully planned for annual conference action on a resolution that had been drafted and approved at the 1966 special session of General Conference and was to be voted on by each annual conference. The resolution was titled, "For The Elimination Of Racial Structure And The Development Of Greater Understanding And Brotherhood In The Methodist Church." (See pages 138-139.)

When the Plan of Union was presented for a vote at the 1967 session of Annual Conference, there was some confusion among the segregationists about the Plan of Union and how it affected segregation. Thus, the Plan of Union passed by the very narrow margin of 281 for union and 269 against. However, when the Resolution for the Elimination of Racial Structure was voted on there was no confusion and the Resolution was soundly defeated 267 against and 207 for.

The difficulty confronted by the Tri-Conference Advisory Committee was that in spite of their best efforts, the Alabama-West Florida Conference voted against every plan of merger submitted by the committee. It was not until 1972 when merger was absolutely mandated by the General Conference, that the Alabama-West Florida Conference finally voted to approve a plan of merger.

The refusal of the Alabama-West Florida Conference to adopt a reasonable and orderly plan of merger was greatly embarrassing to the Church and its leaders. The merger controversy was, likewise, an issue of increased disillusionment to many Methodist ministers. The secular society had long since removed the legal barriers of racial segregation, but the church had failed to do so. So in the late 1960s, a new determination to deal with this cancer in the body of the church was put forward. The concept and approach of voluntarism that the church had so long pursued, and that had proven to be so unsuccessful in eliminating segregation, was being replaced with mandated time limits. However, even at this late date, Alabama Methodists remained resistant.

The movement for black equality and justice may have prevailed in the US courts and in the halls of the US Congress, but in the Methodist Church of the Alabama-West Florida Conference in May of 1967, segregation remained. And, as if to punctuate and emphasize their commitment to continued segregation, the annual conference elected the George C. Wallace, the champion of segregation, as one of its lay delegates to the Dallas Uniting Conference.

RESOLUTION

FOR THE ELIMINATION OF RACIAL STRUCTURE AND THE DEVELOPMENT OF GREATER UNDERSTANDING AND BROTHERHOOD IN THE METHODIST CHURCH

1. By the adoption of this Resolution each Annual Conference, each Jurisdictional Conference, the General Conference, each College of Bishops and the Council of Bishops pledge their best efforts to eliminate as soon as possible all forms of racial structure from the organization of The Methodist Church, and further pledge to do everything possible to develop greater understanding and brotherhood in all aspects of church life and work.

2. Each Annual Conference and Jurisdictional Conference which has been part of a merger of churches or Conferences formerly separated by racial distinctions pledges its best efforts to work out all remaining adjustments, to use the ability of both clergy and laymen wherever they can be most effective in the work of the Church, and to serve all people without regard to race.

Where such mergers have not yet been realized, each such Conference expresses its earnest determination to work toward such merger at the earliest possible date and hereby pledges to establish a Committee on Inter-Conference Relations composed of an equal number of ministers, laymen, and youth to implement the recommendations and resolutions of this report and recommendation of the Plan of Action for the elimination of the Central Jurisdiction adopted by the 1964 General Conference and that each board and agency of the Church be alert for opportunities to assist each Committee in every possible way.

3. Whenever such mergers hereafter take place the continuing Annual Conference will:

a. Accept into its membership, with all the same rights, privileges, status and obligations, all ministerial members (whether on trial or in full connection) appointed to charges located geographically within the continuing Conference, and all ministerial members under special appointment or retired ministerial members who hold Quarterly Conference membership in a local church located geographically within the boundaries of the continuing Conference.

b. Insofar as possible, the ministerial and lay persons now serving on boards and agencies of both the merging Conferences shall serve during the current quadrennium on like or similar boards and agencies of the continuing Conference, and thereafter members in all such Conference boards and agencies shall be open to all persons on the basis of their qualifications without regard to race. In the event any Disciplinary provision limiting the number of members of a current quadrennium, the Cabinet shall determine which members shall continue, in the spirit of this Resolution, being careful to provide for a continuing representation of both of the former Conferences.

c. Within the boundaries of such a continuing Conference opportunities for spiritual and intellectual growth in Christian service shall be made available to all without regard to race or color. Such equal opportunities shall be provided particularly in such aspects of Conference programs as activities of the Woman's Society of Christian Service, Wesleyan Service Guild, youth work, leadership training enterprises and the Board of Lay Activities.

4. Upon the adoption of this Resolution by the requisite vote in the North Carolina-Virginia Conference, each of the Western North Carolina, North Carolina and Virginia Conferences, all of the Annual Conferences of the Central Jurisdiction and all of the Conferences of the Southeastern Jurisdiction, the North Carolina-

Virginia Annual Conference will be dissolved. Each church formerly part of the North Carolina-Virginia Conference shall thereupon be merged with and become part of the other of said Annual Conferences within the geographic bounds of which it is located.

5. Upon the adoption of this Resolution by the requisite vote in the Tennessee-Kentucky Conference, in each of the Holston, Tennessee, Memphis, Kentucky and Louisville Annual Conferences of the Southeastern Jurisdiction, in all of the Annual Conferences of the Central Jurisdiction and in all of the Conferences of the Southeastern Jurisdiction, the Tennessee-Kentucky Annual Conference will be dissolved. Each church formerly part of the Tennessee-Kentucky Conference shall thereupon be merged with and become part of the other of said Annual Conferences within the geographic bounds of which it is located.

6. Upon the adoption of this Resolution by a 2/3rds vote of those present and voting in each of the Louisiana, Southwest, Texas and West Texas Conferences of the Central Jurisdiction, in all of the Annual Conferences of the Central Jurisdiction and in all of the Annual Conferences of the South Central Jurisdiction, the bishop formerly serving the Southwestern Area of the Central Jurisdiction shall be transferred to the South Central Jurisdiction for residential and presidential service, and the Louisiana, Southwest, Texas and West Texas Conferences formerly part of the Central Jurisdiction will be Conferences of the South Central Jurisdiction.

7. Upon the adoption of this Resolution by a 2/3rds vote of those present and voting in each of the Central Alabama, Florida, Georgia, Mississippi, Upper Mississippi and South Carolina Conferences of the Central Jurisdiction and in all of the Annual Conferences of the Central Jurisdiction and all the Annual Conferences of the Southeastern Jurisdiction, the bishops who are then serving the Atlantic Coast and Nashville-Carolina Areas of the Central Jurisdiction shall be transferred to the Southeastern Jurisdiction for residential and presidential service, and the Central Alabama, Florida, Georgia, Mississippi, Upper Mississippi and South Carolina Conferences formerly part of the Central Jurisdiction will be Conferences of the Southeastern Jurisdiction. The transfer and merger of Conferences under paragraphs 4 and 5, and the transfer of Conferences under paragraphs 6 and 7 will be effective upon the close of a special session of the Central Jurisdictional Conference of 1967, and the Central Jurisdiction will thereupon be dissolved.

8. By the adoption of this Resolution by the Southeastern and South Central Jurisdictional Conferences and by the Colleges of Bishops of Southeastern and South Central it is determined that beginning in 1968 the episcopal residences and Areas will be so arranged that no Area will be composed solely of Annual Conferences formerly part of the Central Jurisdiction.

9. By the adoption of this Resolution the Council of Bishops evidences its readiness to transfer bishops across Jurisdictional lines in order to effectuate the purpose of this Resolution, and the bishops individually affirm their readiness to serve wherever they can be of greatest use.

10. By the adoption of this Resolution each Annual Conference, each Jurisdictional Conference, the General Conference, each College of Bishops and the Council of Bishops express their determination to do everything possible to bring about the elimination of any structural organization in The Methodist Church based on race at the earliest possible date and not later than the close of the Jurisdictional Conferences of 1972. They further express their earnest determination to do everything possible to develop greater understanding and brotherhood in Methodism as well as in the world.

MORE DEFECTIONS OVER RACE

The increasing pressure and obvious determination of the Methodist Church to remove the structure and practice of segregation from its life caused a significant increase in the number of members of the Alabama-West Florida Conference who withdrew their membership from the Methodist Church. Between 1955 and 1964 the total membership of the Methodist Church in the Alabama-West Florida Conference experienced a net increase in membership each and every year without exception. During those years the total membership of the conference grew from 124,850 to 130,678, an average net annual growth of 582 additional members each year. However, in the following three years of 1965, 1966, and 1967, total membership declined each year from the previous year. In just those three years the total membership of the conference declined from 130,678 to 128,826. An average net decline of 617 members each year.[11]

Additionally, average weekly attendance at Sunday school experienced year to year growth in every year between 1955 and 1964, increasing during this period from a weekly Sunday school attendance average of 48,348 to a weekly average of 52,135. However, beginning in 1965, and continuing through 1966, and 1967, the weekly Sunday school average attendance decline from 52,135 to 47,874. In just these three years attendance had dropped below the level of ten years earlier.[12] During that same period, the use of unapproved, non-Methodist literature in Sunday school increased from 10 percent to 20 percent of all Sunday school classes. This trend clearly indicated the conflict between the local views on race and other matters of concern and the national church's teachings as stated in Methodist literature.[13]

The passage of time and the accepted racial changes in secular society did little, if anything, to bring acceptance of racial change within the church. Those feelings expressed in November 1963, when the Union Springs Methodist Church officially withdrew from the Methodist church, had not gone away or subsided. While the Union

---

[11]Ibid., 1955-1967, Statistical Tables.
[12]Ibid.
[13]Ibid., 1967, 85.

Springs Church and the Trinity Methodist Church in Mobile were the only two congregations to officially withdraw from the Methodist Church, many individual members withdrew their membership over the issue of race.

Independent Methodist Churches were organized in a number of communities from dissident, disaffected Methodist members. Such churches were organized in Centreville, Greenville, Mobile, Selma, Montgomery, and elsewhere. Nevertheless, there is no statistical data that can adequately and meaningfully convey the real damage done to the church, its clergy, and its faithful members by the long years of accommodation and silence, those years when the church bell failed to ring.

11

AGONIZING AND DEFINING
DECISIONS: 1968-1972

The minister is the only professional, with the exception of the professional golfer, who is expected by his clientele to deal exclusively with the white community. A white doctor may minister to the medical needs of a black; a white lawyer may represent a black at the bar of justice; but woe to the white minister who attempts to meet the religious needs of a black.

—Charles M. Prestwood
A New Breed Of Clergy

IN 1968, AFTER SIXTEEN AND A HALF YEARS AS A PARISH MINISTER OF THE Methodist Church, I left the Methodist Church and its ministry. With a wife and four children and no other means of support I informed the Bishop that I would no longer take an appointment as minister of a United Methodist Church. My family relocated to Seattle, Washington, and I went back to school in preparation for a new career as an investment banker. Twenty-three years later in 1992, I retired from First Interstate Bank of Washington, after having risen to the position of the senior manager of the three billion dollar personal trust division of the bank. When I left the ministry at the end of 1968 it was a very difficult, deliberate, and painful decision, one that I had struggled and agonized over in the prior few years. But my decision was not a unique one.

Literally scores of young men had been making similar decisions in the arduous racial-crisis years of the 1950s and 1960s. As I mentioned at the beginning of this book, between 1950 and 1955, 101 young men entered the Methodist parish ministry in the Alabama-West Florida Conference. Of that 101, 41.6 percent had left the ministry and/or the Alabama-West Florida Conference by 1968. In addition, many more who had joined the conference either prior to 1950 or subsequent to 1955 also left the ministry during these years.

Then in the 1968 to 1970 period the floodgates of attrition broke wide open. The cumulative, eroding impact of the years of racial crisis and the disillusioning awareness of the impotence of the institutional church to positively respond in principle to this challenge became a watershed issue for many. The dimension of the clergy exodus in the twelve months from May 1968 to May 1969 was so significant, and portended such staggering implications for the future ministry of the Alabama-West Florida Conference, that the Board of Pastoral Care and Counseling presented as part of its report to the 1969 Annual Conference, the following:

> The Area Board Executive Committee in its recent meeting spent considerable time studying with sadness and growing alarm the increasing number of men who are leaving the pastoral ministry. The seriousness of this trend places a growing urgency upon . . . the Bishop and the Cabinet as they take needed administrative steps to combat this crisis. . . .
>
> There seems to have swept over us all at this Annual Conference Session a shocking awareness of what has been happening to the ministry in the past twelve months, and a fearful projection of what will happen over the next twelve months if this trend continues . . . The rate of attrition by any standards certainly warrants the kind of pervading shock and concern that has been felt and expressed here this week.
>
> An unofficial and casual survey of the losses we have sustained from May 27th of 1968 through May 27th of 1969 indicates that we have lost from the pastoral ministry of this Conference, other than by death and normal retirement, some thirty-five ministers, which is more than the numerical equivalent of one of the nine Districts. . . . This is almost 20% (18.89% to be exact) of all the seminary graduates serving in the pastoral ministry in this Conference. These thirty-five persons range in age from the early twenties through the mid-fifties; with the largest number falling between ages twenty-eight and thirty-six. They range in number of service years of from one to thirty-three. . . . WE CAN ILL-AFFORD ANOTHER TWELVE MONTHS WITH AN ATTRITION RATE LIKE THAT.[1]

---

[1]*Journal of the Alabama-West Florida Conference, The United Methodist Church*, 1969, 181.

This alarming report did not seek to identify the reasons for this phenomenal attrition, but it did call on the leadership and the entire conference to focus on this crisis, to stem the hemorrhaging loss of its clergy. The attrition continued for the next two years with an additional fifteen ministers leaving in 1969, and another twelve departing in 1970.[2]

High among the list of factors for the exodus was the Church's inability and unwillingness to pay the price in lost revenue and members in order to open its doors and welcome everyone to its services without regard to race. Another dominant factor was the conflict that frequently developed between the minister and his parishioners on these issues which were a matter of principle to many ministers. Yet another factor was the perceived failure of conference leaders from the bishop on down to take positive stands and to provide support for those ministers who, in following their conscience, took unpopular positions. These and many other personal factors simply reached the point of finality for many of these departing ministers.

For these ministers the continued pastoral ministry in the Methodist Church of the Alabama-West Florida Conference was no longer a positive, constructive option in their personal and professional lives. The personal disruption, the economic insecurity, and the family dislocation involved made these decisions exceedingly difficult. However, all these factors personally were more manageable than the continuation of a ministry that for them had reached a point of crisis and diminishing returns.

ENDING SEGREGATION: THE 1968 GENERAL CONFERENCE

While these scores of men were leaving the Alabama-West Florida Conference and the pastoral ministry, the Methodist Church finally addressed in a determined, mandatory way the ending of structural segregation within the church. After years of lofty pronouncements that failed to alter the status quo, change was finally in the air.

---

[2]Ibid., 1969, 1970.

Change in all around we see is both lyric and fact. To any careful observer of the life of The United Methodist Church, this axiom is also the prudent estimate of our condition.

The churches forming The United Methodist Church—The Evangelical United Brethren Church and The Methodist Church—bear the marks of change.[3]

With these words from the Episcopal Greeting the uniting General Conference of the United Methodist Church was opened in Dallas, Texas in April 1968. The Conference lived up to this description of change. A new constitution was adopted. New structures and new policies were approved. Two major denominations with historic experiences and traditions bridged their differences and joined together to become the largest Protestant denomination of that time. But the most profound of all the changes was the final elimination of the Central Jurisdiction, the all-black jurisdiction that had haunted and segregated ministers, churches, and conferences on the basis of race since the 1939 merger that created the Methodist Church.

Beginning in 1956, every session of the quadrennial General Conference had wrestled with the problem of eliminating the Central Jurisdiction. In fact, this issue had been the most dominant matter debated and discussed at the 1956, the 1960, and the 1964 General Conference sessions.[4] Various proposals and constitutional amendments had been presented to the general church for approval, but every proposal and amendment had been based on voluntarism. Now, the urgency of the church's failure to positively address this emotionally-charged issue turned to mandatory actions. With the adoption of the new, uniting church constitution, the Central Jurisdiction ceased to exist.[5]

---

[3]The Book of Discipline, The United Methodist Church (Nashville: Methodist Publishing House, 1968), v.

[4]Based on a careful review of the Daily Proceedings included in Journal of the General Conference, The Methodist Church (Nashville: The Methodist Publishing House, 1956, 1960, 1964).

[5]The constitution was adopted in Chicago, Illinois, on 11 November, 1966, by the General Conferences of the Evangelical United Brethren Church and the Methodist Church and thereafter by the requisite vote in the annual conferences of the two churches. The Plan of Union was made effective by the Uniting Conference in Dallas, Texas, on 23 April, 1968. Discipline, 17.

The practical effect of this mandated change was to immediately take each black annual conference that had made up the Central Jurisdiction and merge it into the geographic jurisdiction in which it resided. This meant that in Alabama, for example, the Central Alabama Conference (the all-black conference) was now a part of the Southeastern Jurisdiction.

Therefore, the state of Alabama would have three Methodist annual conferences. The North Alabama Annual Conference consisted of all the white churches and ministers in the northern half of the state; the Alabama-West Florida Annual Conference consisted of all the white churches and ministers in the southern half of Alabama and the pan-handle of Florida; and the Central Alabama Conference consisted of all the black churches and ministers in the geographic bounds of the two white conferences. In other words, segregation remained, but the first layer of segregated structure, the all-black Central Jurisdiction had been eliminated. This was step one taken by the 1968 Uniting General Conference to end structural segregation.

The second, and more difficult step in the elimination of racial segregation in the United Methodist Church was the merging of the black annual conferences into the white annual conferences in which they geographically resided. To accomplish this mandated step the 1968 General Conference granted each annual conference involved a four year time span, until 1972, to work out the details of merger, but swift action was encouraged and hoped for.

In Alabama, Bishop W. Kenneth Goodson delegated the responsibility of working out the details and conflicts of merger to an appointed Tri-Conference Advisory Committee chaired by Reverend Paul Duffey. This committee composed of representatives of all three Alabama Conferences was charged with presenting a specific plan of merger to the next annual conference (1969) of each of the three merging conferences.

PREPARING THE PLAN OF MERGER

Duffey and the other members of the Tri-Conference Advisory Committee were faced with no small task. The membership of the Alabama-West Florida Conference had, over the years, manifested a determined resistance to any change in its racial policies and behavior.

The mandatory action of the 1968 General Conference notwithstanding, there was no clear evidence that the resistance had diminished.

From its first organizing meeting on April 7, 1967, the Tri-Conference Advisory Committee established a dual-tract approach to its mission.[6] They perceived their first task as one of communication and education, and only after this first step was effectively pursued would other steps follow.

Step two was the development of a specific plan of merger between the conferences and a fixed time table for its implementation. Details about clerical credential qualifications had to be resolved as did major differences in the financial structures of the three conferences. Substantial disparity between the minimum salary schedules and the pension benefit rates and funding levels of the conferences had to be made uniform with adequate funding structures established.

Because these issues as well as several other challenges required practical and difficult solutions, the committee decided that their Plan of Merger would be presented to the 1969 session of the Alabama-West Florida Conference, but a vote to approve the plan would not be taken until the 1970 session.[7]

Two years of preparation in developing the Plan of Merger and an additional year of education, discussion, and promotion at the district and local church level proved to be insufficient. Even when faced with a mandated date of 1972 to adopt and implement a Plan of Merger, the membership of the Alabama-West Florida Conference was simply determined to resist any change in its racial structure and policy. On June 3, 1970, when the Plan of Merger was presented to the annual conference members for a vote, it was defeated 369 against to 297 for.

The defeat was a further embarrassment to Bishop Goodson, a distressing frustration to the Tri-Conference Advisory Committee, and a loud, ugly message to the ministers and churches of the Central Alabama Conference. Particularly sensitive to the impact of this decision on the Central Alabama Conference which was scheduled to vote on the Plan of Merger at its June, 1970, Annual session,[8] Goodson sent Joel McDavid, a leading minister of the Alabama-West

---

[6]Bishop Paul A. Duffey, written interview, 22 April 1994.
[7]*Journal of the Alabama-West Florida Conference*, 1970, 144-146.
[8]Ibid., 1970.

Florida Conference to meet with the Central Alabama Conference. McDavid said of this matter:

> I did all I could to assist in the merger. I spoke on the Annual Conference floor strongly in favor of it. But it was turned down and then Bishop Goodson asked me to go to the black [Central Alabama] Annual Conference as a fraternal delegate and speak to them about the efforts we were making.

McDavid continued:

> In all this you may be sure that I received the ugly telephone calls, many of them at 3:00 a.m., received ugly letters that called me names and that I will not include in this account, and had some ugly confrontations with people [who opposed the merger].[9]

At the 1970 annual session of the Central Alabama Conference where McDavid took the bishop's fraternal greetings and the report of the Alabama West-Florida Conference's vote was discussed, the delegates voted overwhelmingly to approve the Plan of Merger.

RESISTANT TO THE END

The extent to which the Alabama-West Florida Conference was out of step with the United Methodist Church at large and with the Christian principle of inclusiveness was seen in the endless and fruitless resistance which it demonstrated. After the 1970 defeat of the Plan of Merger, the Tri-Conference Advisory Committee resumed meeting in an effort to find a way to secure the required conference approval of the Plan of Merger. Another year of district and local church meetings were conducted to educate and hopefully persuade the full conference membership that the Plan of Merger should be approved.

When the 1971 session of the Alabama-West Florida Annual Conference met at Huntingdon College in Montgomery June 1, to

---

[9]Bishop Joel McDavid, written interview, 27 April, 1994. McDavid was a member of the Alabama-West Florida Conference from 1944 until his election as a bishop of the United Methodist Church in 1972. McDavid retired in 1984.

June 5, the major item on the agenda was a discussion and vote on the Plan of Merger. Once again led by the chairman of the Tri-Conference Committee, Reverend Paul Duffey, the Plan of Merger was discussed in detail and passionately debated. A secret ballot vote was taken and for the second consecutive year it was defeated, this time by a vote of 324 against and 302 votes for.[10] The General Conference could establish deadline dates and mandate an end to segregated conferences, the Tri-Conference Advisory Committee could draft a Plan of Merger and plead for its acceptance, but the determined will of the Alabama-West Florida Conference to resist the inevitability of change remained constant.

Yet, even the most determined resistance cannot forever hold back the clock nor forestall the inevitable. Thus, when the delegates to the 1972 session of the Alabama-West Florida Conference convened on 28 May 1972, Reverend John Vickers stood before the Conference and said, ". . . the question of merger is no longer a question, as the General Conference said merger will become effective . . . We will adopt a plan of merger or an arbitration board will come give us a plan."[11]

Vickers, who had been the pastor of Governor George Wallace and one of his strongest supporters, had for many years been one of the staunchest opponents of a desegregated church and society. But like many others who had opposed the elimination of segregation, he faced the reality of a mandated change. So in this last and final year in which the conference had the opportunity to vote on the Plan of Merger, practical reality became the order of the day. When the Plan of Merger was presented to the conference for a vote, it passed 393 in favor of the Plan of Merger to 182 against.[12] Eight full years after the secular society had fully desegregated all public facilities, the United Methodist Church finally ended its century long history of segregated church structures.

A special merger session of the three Alabama Conferences was held in Birmingham, Alabama, on 24 October 1972. Presided over by Alabama's new bishop, Carl J. Sanders, the merger session celebrated

---

[10]*Journal of the Alabama-West Florida Conference*, 1971, 93-95.
[11]Ibid., 1972, 78.
[12]Ibid., 83-84.

the history and accomplishments of each of the three conferences. Then Bishop Sanders declared:

> As Resident Bishop of the Birmingham Area of the United Methodist Church I do, on behalf of all the United Methodists in the Birmingham Area declare that the Plan of Merger as presented by the Tri-Conference Advisory Committee has been approved by a majority vote of the members of the three annual conferences present and voting thereon.
>
> I further declare that the Alabama-West Florida Annual Conference, the Central Alabama Annual Conference, and the North Alabama Annual Conference are now merged into two new Annual Conferences to be known as the Alabama-West Florida Annual Conference and the North Alabama Annual Conference.[13]

Following Bishop Sanders's declaration officially merging the black Central Alabama Annual Conference into the two white conferences, all delegates stood and sang the all-inclusive hymn of John Oxenham, *In Christ There Is No East or West*:

> In Christ there is no east or west,
> In him no north or south;
> But one great fellowship of love
> Throughout the whole wide earth . . .
>
> Join hands, then, brothers of the faith,
> What e're your race may be.
> Who serves my Father as a son
> Is surely kin to me.[14]

Weary from years of conflict over the issue of a segregated church, the United Methodist Church of Alabama in 1972 turned with resignation and accepted the inevitable. The long and often bitter struggle between clergy, laity, local church, and national church was

---

[13]From the official program of the United Merger Session, Birmingham area, The United Methodist Church, 24 October, 1972, 4.

[14]Hymn No. 192 in *The Methodist Hymnal* (Nashville: The Methodist Publishing House, 1964).

over. Segregation within the Alabama-West Florida Conference came to an end.

12

THE CHURCH BELL RINGS!
1973-1997

Don't you hear the bells now ringing?
Don't you hear the angels singing?
'Tis the glory hallelujah jubilee!

—Dion de Marbelle

LOOKING FROM 1997 BACKWARD ACROSS A TWENTY-FIVE YEAR experience of black and white Methodists together, one sees a mixed and ambivalent record. The merger of black and white Methodists was not without difficulties, failures, and disappointments, but it was a period of new beginnings.[1]

In a special service of union held at Birmingham-Jefferson Civic Center on 24 October 1972, twenty-one black pastoral charges which lay within the bounds of the Alabama-West Florida Conference officially were integrated with the 366 white pastoral charges. Likewise the thirty active and retired black ministers within those bounds were joined with the 528 active and retired white ministers; and the 3,516 black church members were joined with the 122,593 white church members to form the newly integrated Alabama-West

---

[1]The twenty-five year record of blacks and whites together in the Alabama-West Florida Conference reported in this chapter is based on written and telephone interviews with twenty ministers who are members of the Alabama-West Florida Conference; and on official documents, conference journals, and statistical records kept by the conference. The twenty ministers I interviewed are Floyd Enfinger, Ralph Hendricks, Joe Neal Blair, Charles Britt, Arthur Carlton, Paul Duffey, Langdon Garrison, John Lane, James Love, Joel McDavid, Stanley Mullins, Spencer Turnipseed, Tom Butts, Henry Roberts, Dallas Blanchard, Steve Collins, Robert Collins, O. C. Brown, Don Brown, and Syd Locke. I made an effort to interview eight different black ministers and laymen, but they all declined to be interviewed, including the current bishop.

Florida Conference (see demographics of black churches on next page).[2]

Though far from easy, this was a hopeful and challenging time for white or black Methodists. No longer was any Methodist church, minister, or member a part of a legally-structured segregated institution. Every time the church doors were opened, every time a group of youth, or women, or men, or congregations met, both black and white were to be inclusively welcomed. That was the structure. That was the ideal.

IMPACT ON BLACK METHODISTS

Not surprisingly, black ministers and members experienced the greatest adjustments. In their former black separate conference many opportunities for leadership were available. They had their own district superintendents, their own delegates to General and Jurisdictional Conferences, their own chairmen of boards and agencies. After union, however, they were a very small minority in a dominantly white conference and such leadership opportunities were few. As one white minister put it, "This is not merger, it is absorption!"[3]

In their former Central Alabama Conference they had pastoral opportunities throughout the entire state of Alabama and northwest Florida. That included 49 pastoral charges that were now a part of the North Alabama Conference. Thus, within the newly merged conference there were only twenty-one black pastoral charges available to them in the Alabama-West Florida, unless the bishop, his cabinet of district superintendents, and the white local pastoral charges were open to accepting a black pastor. Unfortunately, the record shows that such was not the case. [4] (See complete list of black pastoral charges on facing page.)

---

[2]*Journal of the Central Alabama Conference*, 1972, 31-33; *Journal of the Alabama West Florida Conference*, 1972, 104-115, Statistical Tables, 106; *The Issues Before Us*, Pamphlet published by the Advisory Committee on Interconference Relations.

[3]Dallas Blanchard. This was part of a statement made during the 1972 Annual Conference debate on merger.

[4]*Journal of the Alabama-West Florida Conference*, 1972-1996.

Churches of the Central Jurisdiction
WITHIN THE BOUNDS OF THE ALABAMA-WEST FLORIDA CONFERENCE
THE METHODIST CHURCH

◆ Number of Churches — 47
Pastoral Charges — 21
Total Members 3,516

——————————————— OTHER FACTS ———————————————

Pastors — 21		Ministers in Special Appointments — 4
Retired Ministers — 3	District Superintendents — 2	Ministers in Full Connection — 19

PRINTED BY THE BOARD OF CHRISTIAN SOCIAL CONCERNS
ALABAMA-WEST FLORIDA CONFERENCE, THE METHODIST CHURCH

BLACK PASTORAL CHARGES, ALABAMA-WEST FLORIDA CONFERENCE

ANDALUSIA DISTRICT
St. Paul Circuit (Evergreen)
St. Paul
Sand Bar
Shiloh
Sparta Hill (Evergreen)

DEMOPOLIS DISTRICT
Akron Circuit
Clark Chapel
Jackson Chapel
Johnson Hill
St. Matthew

Butler Circuit
St. Mary
St. Paul
Wesley Chapel
Montgomery
Metropolitan

Eutaw Circuit
St. Paul
Mt. Sinai
St. Paul
Springfield

Geiger Circuit
Mt. Moriah
Oak Grove
Soul Chapel

Marion Circuit
Antioch
Simpson Chapel
Zion Chapel

Oak Grove Circuit

MOBILE DISTRICT
Toulminville-Warren St.
Wesley Chapel-Theodore
Theodore First
Wesley Chapel

MONTGOMERY DISTRICT
Benson Circuit
Benson
Bethel
Chapel
Rivers Chapel

Eclectic Circuit
Cedar Grove
Oak Valley
St. Paul

Wetumpka: New Style

Opelika: St. Paul

Tuskegee: Bowen

PENSACOLA DISTRICT
Pensacola: St. Paul
Tensaw: Little Zion

Marietta
Oak Grove

DOTHAN DISTRICT	SELMA DISTRICT
No black charges	New Style-Locust
	Locust Bluff
	New Style

MARIANNA DISTRICT	TROY DISTRICT
No black charges	Union Springs:
	St. Paul
	Brown Grove

More critically, the black ministers' career opportunities and ministry potential were severely reduced unless and until white congregations were more than just theoretically open to them as pastoral appointments. In the twenty-five years since the 1972 merger of black and white conferences not even one black minister has ever been appointed as the pastor of a white congregation. And only recently at the First United Methodist Church in Pensacola, Florida, has the first black been appointed as an associate minister.[5] I discussed this essential issue of the openness of white congregations to black ministers with six district superintendents who served in the bishop's appointment making cabinet during those years. In each case they informed me that throughout the years after merger, there was never a discussion of or a consideration given to appointing a black minister to a white congregation.[6] They simply rotated the black ministers among the various black charges.

It is difficult to believe that there were no black ministers who were qualified and capable of pastoring a predominantly white congregation. It is just as difficult to imagine, in those changing times, that not even one white congregation out of the 366 white pastoral charges in the conference would be willing to accept a black minister or a black associate minister. Yet such was the case.

---

[5]Reverend Henry Roberts, written interview, 2 May 1997.

[6]Two of the six district superintendents asked that their names not be used and so I will list none of the six. Their interview records are in my files.

This failure of the Alabama-West Florida Conference to prepare for and to make the opportunities for ministry to any congregation, white or black, available to the black ministers as it did to all white ministers, was a failure that ran totally contrary to the spirit and purpose of the original Plan of Merger.

When the white and black leaders of the Tri-Conference Commission on Merger worked together on a mutually acceptable and workable plan of merger, two critical and key points were made clear concerning the black ministers. The plan said, "within the new conference, opportunities for service shall be made available to all without regard to race or color." Even more specifically the plan said, "With merger, the bishop is urged to consider the appointment of at least one minister from the Central Alabama Conference to the position of District Superintendent."[7]

The reality is that during the twenty-five years of the merged conferences, not only has a black minister never been appointed as pastor of a white congregation but no black minister was or had ever been appointed by the bishop as a district superintendent until June 1997, when the first black, Reverend Warren G. Booker Jr., was appointed as district superintendent of the Mobile District.[8] It took a full twenty-five years for the bishop to fulfill the suggestion of the original Plan of Merger. Not surprisingly, therefore, within the first few years of the 1972 merger of the black and white conferences, many of the most qualified black ministers left the Alabama-West Florida Conference, transferring to other conferences that offered them better and more equal opportunities.

The attrition rate of the black ministers in the Alabama-West Florida Conference was painfully substantial. Of the twenty-two active, appointed black ministers at the time of merger in 1972, nine left the conference in the first five years.[9] Ten years after merger, in 1982, an additional five of the original twenty-two had also left. Thus, within the first ten years following merger, fourteen out of the original

---

[7]*Journal of the Alabama-West Florida Conference*, 1970, 144-146.

[8]*Christian Advocate*, 25 May 1997, 2.

[9]Each of the twenty black pastoral charges had a black minister appointed to it, and in addition one black minister was appointed to a bureaucratic position on the Conference Council.

twenty-two black ministers who became a part of the Alabama-West Florida Conference had left the conference for other opportunities.[10]

Most of the black ministers who left were the fully ordained ministers in full connection with the conference. As they left they were replaced with unordained, part time local pastors.[11] As one of the district superintendents said of this matter, "any black pastor of promise . . . left us. We have very few fully ordained black clergy at the present time. Probably less than ten. Mostly they are part time local pastors."[12] A white minister with 43 years of service in the conference, and who had been a part of the conference leadership, said much the same thing. "Most of the best black ministers," he said, "either went to the General Boards of the church, or to other more 'friendly' conferences."[13] Whatever the reasons, and they undoubtedly are varied and complex, the ending of legal segregation and the merging of the black and white conferences of Alabama resulted in substantially reduced opportunity for the black clergy.

It is somewhat more difficult to evaluate the impact and effect of merger on the local black congregations. The one thing that is clear is that they did not experience any growth in membership even when the white membership was growing. Indeed, the black membership actually showed a small decline.

Over the years of the merged conferences, the white Methodist membership has grown 11.4 percent while the black Methodist membership has declined 3.5 percent. Many factors are obviously involved in this mixed story of merger, but clearly the results are not positive for the black Methodist churches of Alabama. One of the most serious problems impacting the black churches is the fact that most of them are served by part-time, marginally-qualified ministers. Of the twenty-one black charges, in 1996 thirteen of those charges were being served by part-time ministers who were available only on Sundays to conduct worship service, and most of these part time ministers did not even live in the communities where the churches

---

[10]*Journal of the Alabama-West Florida Conference*, 1972, 1977, 1982.
[11]Ibid., 1972-1982.
[12]Reverend Langdon Garrison, written interview, 19 May 1997.
[13]Reverend Syd Lock, written interview, 17 June 1997.

they served were located.[14] It is little wonder that black Methodists membership is not growing in Alabama.

In Methodist conferences all across America, when there are shortages of qualified clergy, the leadership of those conferences actively recruit and develop programs and opportunities to attract qualified clergy to their area. There is no evidence that the leadership of the Alabama-West Florida Conference has ever attempted to develop and promote opportunities even to retain its qualified black clergy, much less to attract additional black clergy. One simple example that just occurred at the 1997 session of annual conference illustrates how little has been done in this area over the years.

It is a long standing historic tradition of the United Methodist Church for each local charge to provide a home called a parsonage for the minister to live in while he or she serves that charge. The minister lives in it rent free and all maintenance and repair is the responsibility of the charge. As long ago as the 1950s, the all-white Alabama-West Florida Conference established minimum standards for parsonages that each church was expected to meet.[15] Yet at the 1997 session of the Annual Conference a special offering was taken to ". . . construct and improve the parsonages in the Demopolis District. The district hopes to raise money to build at least five parsonages for African-American churches."[16] Reverend Charles Walker, district superintendent of the Demopolis District said, "There are eighteen African-American churches served by eight pastors that do not have livable parsonages. The need is great to furnish parsonages for these pastors."[17]

It is very difficult to understand why it has taken twenty-five years for this issue to be addressed, and, of course, the Demopolis District is not the only district that has substandard housing for its black ministers. It would almost seem that a policy of benign neglect has been operating all these years and the net effect is the loss of its best black ministers and a decline in its black membership.

---

[14]Ibid., 1996, Appointment record and Clergy Roll.
[15]Ibid., 1959.
[16]*Christian Advocate*, 25 May 1997, 7.
[17]Ibid.

As one looks back at the opportunities and challenges that were inherent in the 1972 merger of the white and black conferences, it would appear that, at best, inadequate preparation was made and implementation plans were lacking. The clear absence of a positive program focused on putting into effect the details of the Plan of Merger certainly contributed to the less than satisfactory results we see in 1997. When coupled with the residual effects of the many years of intransigent resistence that the Alabama-West Florida Conference had demonstrated toward this issue, it is not surprising that the hopeful seeds of inclusiveness and welcome were planted on barren soil. This is seen not only in the loss of the best of the black clergy and the decline in black membership, but it is dramatically revealed in the white church's flight from almost every changing, transitional neighborhood.

WHITE FLIGHT TO THE SUBURBS

Though the Alabama-West Florida Conference is predominantly a rural and small town conference, it does have a number of urban centers such as Montgomery, Mobile, Pensacola, Panama City, and Selma. Over the last quarter century the neighborhood patterns of these urban centers have changed dramatically just as they have all across America. Many communities which had been exclusively or nearly all-white for decades, began changing to mixed neighborhoods, and finally to predominantly black neighborhoods. Well-established United Methodist Churches with long years of ministry to these local vicinities had an excellent opportunity to reach out and extend ministry to the newer, black residents of those old established neighborhoods. The sad record of the United Methodist Church in these urban centers of the Alabama-West Florida Conference is that it took flight to the suburbs to follow its fleeing members.

Reverend Jim Love describes one of these early flights in the Mobile area in 1976 just four years after merger. He was the minister of the First United Methodist Church in Prichard. Love describes the situation at Prichard: "It was a beautiful church building but a declining congregation located in what is now a predominantly black city adjacent to Mobile." He then goes on to say, "the church simply would not consider opening up to blacks, always referring to 'what happened at Toulminville,' when the subject was brought up." The reference to Toulminville refers all the way back to 1965-1968, when the Warren Street Methodist Church (black) and the Toulminville Methodist Church (white) were merged together (see chapter 10 for details) and almost all of the white members withdrew from the merged church.

Love then continues by saying sadly, "[A]s a result, the church was closed and the property sold . . . The money was turned over to the Mobile District Board of Missions and Church Extension."[18] The opportunity for a local church to reach out and minister to a changing community was lost, and the conference leadership from the bishop to the district superintendent was willing to sell the property and close its Prichard ministry.

During the same general period, two well-established Methodist churches in Montgomery, Frazer Memorial United Methodist Church and St. Mark's United Methodist Church, which had for many decades served stable white middle-class neighborhoods, were suddenly confronted with communities which were rapidly changing from white to black. Instead of closing their churches as Prichard had done, these two Montgomery churches both chose to sell their properties to black congregations and relocate out in the "safe white suburbs."

In both Montgomery and Mobile these decisions were just the beginning of closure and flight to the white suburbs. Three more churches closed in Mobile over the next several years: Oakdale United Methodist Church, Broad Street United Methodist Church, and St. Francis Street United Methodist Church all closed as their neighborhoods changed and their white membership moved to the suburbs. The one bright spot in these closures was when the Mobile District decided to use the physical facilities of St. Francis Street United Methodist Church for its Inner City Ministry. Every week the Inner City Ministry advertises in the local newspaper a "Sunday morning multi-racial, multi-cultural service." Throughout the week the Inner City Ministry also conducts a social service ministry to the community.[19]

---

[18]Reverend James Love, written interview, 7 June 1997.

[19]Garrison, written interview, 19 May 1997; Dr. Dallas Blanchard, written interview, 24 April 1997.

White flight continued also in Montgomery. The relocation of Frazer Memorial and St. Mark's was followed by Asbury United Methodist Church, Forrest Avenue United Methodist Church, and St. James United Methodist Church all selling their church properties and relocating their churches in the white suburbs of Montgomery. Additionally Burge Memorial United Methodist Church simply closed as Prichard, Oakdale, and Broad Street had.[20]

The minister at Asbury United Methodist Church in Montgomery recalls "one Sunday when an attractive young black mother with her child came to church. It happened to be communion Sunday and they came to the altar for communion. After church that day, one of my members asked me 'What did they come here for?'" The minister responded, "They came here to worship with us."[21] A few years after this minister was reassigned, the Asbury church relocated to Narrow Lane Road in a totally white neighborhood. Ironically, that neighborhood is now becoming interracial. The former minister said of the situation, "It is ironic that with blacks now moving into that community, the church is in decline again. If they would open their doors to all in the community they could possibly become a thriving church again."[22]

There are other examples of the Methodist Church fleeing to the white suburbs or closing its doors when blacks move into the neighborhood. There have been at least twelve such closures or moves since the merger of the black and white conferences in 1972. It would surely appear that the United Methodist Church of Alabama has not found a way, or perhaps even a willingness, to experiment, to take risks, to develop new ministries to the blacks of Alabama. One could argue that the blacks themselves do not want to worship with whites, that their cultural differences and religious worship forms are enough different that white and black will always choose to worship separately. Blacks may also choose to worship separately because they are more comfortable worshiping with other blacks and because in a black

---

[20]Bishop Paul Duffey, written interview, 17 June 1997; Reverend Stanley Mullins, telephone interview, 24, 28 May 1997; Lock, written interview, 21 June 1997; personal knowledge of author whose home was Montgomery.

[21]Reverend James Love, interview, 7 June 1997.

[22]Ibid.

church they are in charge. While this may be true to some degree, the argument begs the question. The real question is, has the United Methodist Church reached out in its ministry to include and welcome blacks, including different forms of worship opportunities? Have they developed programs and ministries designed to include the full participation of blacks? Reverend Stanley Mullins, a member of the conference for forty-one years, probably expressed it most pointedly when he said, "While merger took place in 1972, I do not know of any 'educational' programs that took place to prepare the blacks for the shock of becoming a very small part of an all white conference in which they would be lost in the crowd." He quickly added, "I also know of no program of recruitment that has taken place to increase either the lay or ministerial membership of black members."[23]The record of the last twenty-five years certainly seems to verify Mullins' observations quite clearly.

THE POSITIVE DIMENSIONS OF INTERRACIAL MINISTRY

The twenty-five year portrait of black and white in the Alabama-West Florida Conference of the United Methodist Church is far poorer than would be hoped for. The loss of most of the qualified black ministers, the loss of black membership in a growing conference, the closing of a number of churches and the fleeing of other churches to all-white suburbs when neighborhoods experience racial change are all disturbing matters that reflect great need for bi-racial work. Yet, it would be unfair and inaccurate to not also see that the merged conference has experienced some positive dimensions of racial inclusiveness.

From the very beginning of the merged conferences there was an open acceptance and welcome of blacks at church-sponsored functions beyond the local church. Easy integration of blacks and whites occurred at district meetings of youth, or district Women's Society of Christian Service meetings, or at Senior Assembly, or at annual conference, or at various group church activities held at Blue Lake, the conference assembly campground. As Reverend Charles Britt observed regarding this level of racial inclusiveness, "There is a high degree of

---

[23]Mullins, written interview, 19 May 1997.

openness . . . at the conference level. By this I mean attendance at Blue Lake, Huntingdon College, and other places . . . like District meetings."[24] Reverend John Lane concurred, saying, "Blacks have been well accepted on the District and Conference level."[25] This point was stressed in almost every interview I conducted. Clearly, the district and conference gatherings were easily integrated.

The same open acceptance was also experienced at the various bureaucratic positions of the conference as well as on the conference boards and agencies. At the very first annual conference following merger, one of the leading black clergymen was appointed to a bureaucratic leadership position on the Conference Council. The various bureaucrats on the council not only hold conference positions of leadership, but each of the six members of the 1973 Conference Council had specific areas of responsibility. Reverend E. D. Ridgeway, who had been the district superintendent of the Montgomery District of the Central (black) Alabama Conference at the time of merger, was appointed to the Conference Council. His major responsibility was to serve as liaison between the newly merged black churches, ministers, and members and the white churches, ministers, and members. Ridgeway served in this position until his retirement in 1983. Three years later in 1986 another black minister, Terrence K. Hayes, was appointed to the same Conference Council position and served in that capacity until 1989 when he accepted a position out of the conference as a bureaucrat with the General Board of Discipleship.

In recent years Edna Williams, a black woman, has served on the Conference Council of Ministries, and in the Pensacola District a black, Curtis Henderson, has served as the district lay leader. One of the district superintendents I interviewed told me, "Attempts were made to place representative blacks on all conference boards, committees, and agencies."[26] Most important of all, in 1992 a black bishop, William Wesley Morris, was assigned as resident bishop of the Alabama-West Florida Conference and according to everyone I interviewed, he has been well received throughout the conference.

---

[24]Reverend Charles Britt, written interview, 20 April 1997.
[25]Reverend John Lane, written interview, 5 May 1997.
[26]Garrison, written interview, 19 May 1997.

These efforts for inclusiveness at the ecclesiastical, bureaucratic, and board level have been favorably accepted throughout the conference from the time of merger to the present. But Reverend Floyd Enfinger expressed the view stated by almost all the ministers I interviewed about this twenty-five year period when he said, "In my opinion, the racial relations have improved in our bureaucracy and in our connectional system. But at the grass-root level things are about the same as they have always been."[27]

Fortunately, there are several local formerly all-white congregations that now have one or more black families as members. Based on the best information I could secure,[28] between eight and twelve local churches have black members. Dauphin Way United Methodist Church and the Inner City Mission in Mobile, First United Methodist Church and Frazer Memorial United Methodist Church in Montgomery, First United Methodist Church in Pensacola, First United Methodist Church in Marion, and Barrett Road United Methodist Church in Selma are all churches that have black members. In each case they seem to be welcomed as active participants in all church activities. In all likelihood, several other such churches exist, but considering that the conference in 1997 had 448 white pastoral charges and that the black general population within the bounds of the Alabama-West Florida Conference represents over 30 percent of the total population, then this twenty-five year record should not bring any pride to the Methodists of Alabama-West Florida.

Retired Bishop Paul A. Duffey probably expressed the situation best when he said, "A number of our white congregations have received black members into their churches. The total number is small and there is significant turnover." Duffey continued, "In summary I would say that relationships between black and white members have increased in number and in quality, but participation has declined."[29] In commenting on this same issue Tom Butts is even more forceful

---

[27]Reverend Floyd Enfinger, written interview, 8 June 1997.

[28]The Alabama-West Florida Conference does not keep any official records of the number of churches with black members. The number eight to twelve used in this chapter is based on the best information and personal knowledge of ten different ministers I interviewed.

[29]Duffey, interview, 17 June 1997.

when he says, "Real integration (as opposed to encapsulated absorption) will never happen until someone gets brave enough to appoint a black minister to a significant white congregation." Butts closes his observation by saying, "We are about as racist as we have ever been, but we are more sophisticated about it, which makes the whole thing the more insidious."[30] After twenty-five years of white and black merged conferences, King's statement that "at 11:00 o'clock on Sunday morning . . . we are in the most totally segregated hour of the week" is still true.

---

[30]Dr. Tom Butts, written interview, 24 June 1997.

BIBLIOGRAPHY

A. BOOKS

Anderson, William K. *Methodism*. Nashville: The Methodist Publishing House, 1947.

Bartley, Numan V. *The Rise of Massive Resistance*. Baton Rouge: Louisiana State University Press, 1969.

_____ and Hugh D. Graham. *Southern Politics and the Second Reconstruction*. Baltimore: The John Hopkins University Press, 1975.

Jack Bass. *Unlikely Heroes*. New York: Simon and Schuster, 1981.

_____. *Taming The Storm*. New York: Doubleday, 1993.

Branch, Taylor. *Parting The Waters: America During the King Years*. New York: Simon and Schuster, 1988.

Carson, Clayborne. *In Struggle: SNCC and the Black Awakening of the 1960s*. Cambridge: Harvard University Press, 1981.

Carter, Hodding III. *The South Strikes Back*. New York: Doubleday and Company, Inc., 1959.

Discipline of the Methodist Church. Nashville: The Methodist Publishing House, 1956, 1960, 1964, 1968, 1972.

Dorman, Michael. *The George Wallace Myth*. New York: Bantam Books, 1965.

Fager, Charles E. *Selma 1965*. New York: Charles Scribner's Sons, 1974.

Fairclough, Adam. *To Redeem The Soul of America: The Southern Christian Leadership Conference and Martin Luther King, Jr.* Athens: University of Georgia Press, 1987.

Gross, John O. *The Beginnings of American Methodism*. Nashville: Abingdon Press, 1961.

Harmon, Nolan B. *The Organization of the Methodist Church*. Nashville: The Methodist Publishing House, 1962.

Jones, Bill. *The Wallace Story*. Northport, AL: American Southern Publishing Company, 1966.

Journal of the Alabama-West Florida Conference, 1948-1996.

Journal of General Conference of the Methodist Church. Nashville: The Methodist Publishing House.

King, Martin Luther Jr., *Stride Toward Freedom*. New York: Harper and Row, 1958.

Martin Luther King, Jr. Why We Can't Wait. New York: Harper and Row, 1963.

Lewis, David Levering. *King: A Critical Biography*. New York: Praeger Publishers, 1970.

Martin, John Bartlow. *The Deep South Says Never*. New York: Ballentine Press, 1957.

The Methodist Hymnal. Nashville: The Methodist Publishing House, 1964.

McLeod, Powers. *Southern Accents, Different Voices*. Pensacola, FL: Ardara House Publishers, 1993.

McMillen, Neil R. *The Citizens' Council*. Urbana: University of Illinois Press, 1971.

Norrell, Robert J. *Reaping the Whirlwind: The Civil Rights Movement in Tuskegee*. New York: Alfred A. Knopf, 1985.

Prestwood, Charles. *The New Breed Clergy*. Grand Rapids: William B. Eerdmans, 1972.

Raines, Howell. *My Soul Is Rested: Movement Days in the Deep South Remembered*. New York: G. P. Putnam's Sons, 1977.

Robinson, Jo Ann Gibson. *The Montgomery Bus Boycott and the Women Who Started It* Knoxville: University of Tennessee Press, 1987.

Sikora, Frank. *The Judge, The Life and Opinions of Alabama's Frank M. Johnson, Jr*. Montgomery, AL: The Black Belt Press, 1992.

Taper, Bernard. *Gomillion versus Lightfoot*. New York: McGraw-Hill, 1962.

Wallace, George C. *Hear Me Out*. Montgomery, AL: Droke House Publishers, 1968.

Washington, James M. *A Testament of Hope: The Essential Writings of Martin Luther King Jr*. New York: Harper and Row, 1986.

Wolff, Miles. *Lunch at the 5 and 10: The Greesboro Sit-ins; A Contemporary History*. Stein and Day, 1970.

Yarbrough, Tinsley E. *Judge Frank Johnson and Human Rights in Alabama*. Tuscaloosa: University of Alabama Press, 1981.

Zellner, James, and others. *Making Methodism Methodist*. Stone and Pierce, 1947.

Zinn, Howard. *SNCC: The New Abolitionists*. New York: Beacon Press, 1964.

B. ARTICLES, JOURNALS, AND PAPERS

Bulletin of the Methodist Laymen's Union.

Cooper, Margaret. Letter to the Reverend Billy Frank Hall, pastor of the Tuskegee Methodist Church, 27 July 1966.

Ellis, Marlene. Letter to the Reverend Billy Frank Hall, pastor of the Tuskegee Methodist Church, 27 July, 1966.

Goodson, W. Kenneth. Letter to all ministers of the Alabama-West Florida and North Alabama Conferences, 1 April, 1965,

Hodge, Backman G. Letter to all ministers and churches of the Alabama West-Florida Conference, 25 March, 1960.

Kennedy, Robert F. Letter to the Reverend Powers McLeod, 9 January 1964, Powers McLeod Personal Papers.

King, Martin Luther Jr. *Letter From Birmingham Jail*. New York: American Friends Service Committee, May 1963.

Nichols, J. B. "A Tragic Era In Our History: The Story of The Methodist Layman's Union." Unpublished article.

Osborne, George R. "Boycott In Birmingham." *The Nation,* 5 May, 1962.

Prestwood, Charles. "The Southern Church, Its Past and Future Hope," Lecture given at Union, Yale, Drew, and Boston Universities.

Purcell, Clair. Letter to the Reverend Ray Whatley, Ray Whatley personal papers.

J. Mills Thornton III, "Challenge and Response in the Montgomery Bus Boycott of 1955-1956," *The Alabama Review* 33 (July 1980).

Turnipseed, Spencer. Speech to Southeastern Jurisdictional Historical Society, 12 July, 1995.

Warren, Richard L. "Birmingham, Brinkmanship in Race Relations", *Christian Century*, 30 May, 1962.

Women's Division of Christian Service. *The Methodist Church and Race*. Nashville: Women's Division of Christian Service, 1962.

C. NEWSPAPERS AND MAGAZINES

The Alabama Journal
The Christian Century
The Methodist Christian Advocate
The Mobile Press Register
The Montgomery Advertiser
The Nation
Newsweek
Time
The Union Springs Herald

D. INTERVIEWS

Atkinson, Reverend W. B. "Jack," 24 August 1993.
Blair, Reverend Joe Neal, 4 October, 1993.
Blanchard, Dr. Dallas, 9 March 1994 and 24 April 1997.
Britt, Reverend Charles, 10 November 1993 and 20 April 1997.
Brown, Reverend O. C., 1994.
Brown, Dr. Don, 1995.
Butts, Reverend Tom, 24 September 1993 and 24 June 1997.
Caddell, Reverend Eugene, 17 September, 1993.
Carlton, Reverend Arthur, 28 March 1994.
Dickerson, Reverend Robert E., 20 July, 1993.
Duffey, Bishop Paul, 22 April 1994; 17 June 1997.
Enfinger, Reverend Floyd, 5 July 1993 and 8 June 1997.
Garrison, Reverend Langdon, 6 January 1994 and 19 May 1997.
Griggs, Reverend William, 1994.
Hale, Reverend Maxwell, 27-28 July 1994.
Hendricks, Reverend Ralph, 14 January 1994.
Henne, Reverend Ed, 14 July 1993.
Lane, Reverend John H., 18 June 1993 and 5 May 1997.
Lindsey, Reverend Warren, 20 April 1994.

Lisenby, Reverend Joseph, 8 December 1993.

Locke, Reverend Syd, 17 June 1997.

Love, Reverend Jim, 8 July 1993 and 7 June 1997.

McDavid, Bishop Joel, 27 April 1994.

McLeod, Reverend L. Powers, 18 June 1993.

Mullins, Reverend Stanley Mullins, 3 November, 1994.

Nichols, J. B., 1 May 1994.

Prestwood, Reverend Dr. Charles numerous person interviews with notes from 1959 to 1968. Robert, Reverend Henry, 2 May 1997.

Rush, Frances, October 1994.

Sellers, Reverend Ennis, 1967.

Shirah, Sam Jr., 1964 and 1965.

Sublette, Reverend Roy T., 24 August, 1994.

Turnipseed, Reverend Dr. Andrew, 1994.

Turnipseed, Reverend Spencer, 8 May 1997.

Whatley, Reverend Ray E., 2 May 1992; 19 May 1992; 8 January 1994; 11 January 1994.

BIBLIOGRAPHY

Abernathy, Ralph, 23, 33

African Methodist Episcopal Church, 2, 103

African Methodist Episcopal Zion Church, 2, 37, 106

Alabama Advisory Committee, 52-54, 60, 117

Alabama-West Florida Conference, xi, 11, 13, 14, 21, 22, 31, 45-47, 54, 58, 62, 65, 69, 70, 78, 97, 100, 120, 136, 144, 147, 151, 154, 158

Atkinson, W.B. Jr., 33, 51

Auburn, ix, 16, 75, 89-92

Birmingham, ix, x, 10, 19, 51, 59, 70, 73, 77, 82, 107, 150

Birmingham-Southern College, 27, 54, 59, 76

Blair, Joe Neal, 17, 32, 66-67 106-107, 117

Blanchard, Dallas, 117, 119-123, 154

Britt, Charles, 66, 164

Butts, Tom, 33, 40-42, 49-50, 74, 129-130, 166

Camden Methodist Church, 104

Carlton, Arthur M., 109

Central Alabama Conference, 120, 136, 139, 147, 151, 154, 158, 165

Central Jurisdiction, 3, 22, 46, 94-96, 120, 135-136, 138-139, 146-147, 155

Dexter Avenue Methodist Church, 11, 27

Doar, John, 53, 90

Douglas, John, 90, 91, 92

Duffey, Bishop Paul A., 26-27, 136, 147, 150, 163, 166

Dumas Bill, 20, 55-56, 57, 59, 60, 84-87

Enfinger, Floyd, 17, 23, 24, 34, 166

Franklin, Harold A., 89-91

Frazer, G. Stanley, 19-20, 22, 25-27, 28, 32, 47, 55

Garrison, Langdon, 41, 66, 159

General Conference, 4, 5, 6, 21, 22, 32, 46, 57, 63-64, 94-97, 98, 134, 135, 138-139

Goodson, Bishop W. Kenneth, 87, 100-101, 105-110, 118, 119-123, 128-129, 136, 147, 148

Greensboro Methodist Church 105-106

Hale, Maxwell, ix, 74, 90-92

Hall, Billy Frank, 131-132

Hardin, Bishop Paul, Jr., 62, 77-78, 85-87, 98-100, 106

Harmon, Bishop Nolan B., 3, 62, 77

Hendricks, Ralph, 105-106, 117

Henne, Ed, 17, 40, 104

Hodge, Bishop Bachman G., 41-44, 46, 54, 56, 59-60, 62

Huntingdon College, 21, 31, 33, 69, 78, 97, 122, 149

Jurisdictional Conference, 3, 4, 5, 22, 100, 138-139

King, Martin Luther Jr., ix, 10, 23, 28, 31, 33, 35, 49, 54, 75, 77, 80-81, 103, 127

Kneel-ins, 65-67, 68, 124, 128-133

Lane John H., 17, 36-38, 51, 165

Lindsey, Warren, 108

Love, Jim, 16, 33, 40-42, 69, 80-81, 161-162, 163

McDavid, Bishop Joel D., 115-116, 148-149

McLeod, Powers, 17, 33, 74, 90-92, 101, 117, 119-120, 129

Marion Methodist Church, 106-107

Maxey, Torrence, 85-86

Methodist Episcopal Church, North, 2

Methodist Episcopal Church, South, 2-3, 11

Methodist Laymen's Union, 19, 22, 55, 57, 59-61, 64, 74, 108, 111, 113

Methodist Protestant Church, 2

Mobile, ix, 36, 39, 51, 75, 82, 131, 132, 141

Montgomery, x, 6, 21, 24, 26, 27, 29, 33, 51, 69, 70, 75, 78, 128, 132, 141, 161

Montgomery Bus Boycott x, 23, 24, 27, 31, 35, 36, 39, 69, 106

Moore, Judge L. S., 32, 47

Mullins, Stanley, 25, 67, 117, 164

NAACP, 15, 36

National Council of Churches, 85, 92, 97-98, 116, 124

Nichols, J. B., 54, 58-59, 67, 106, 117

North Alabama Conference, 11, 62, 100, 136, 147, 151, 154

Parker, John, 40-43

Pensacola, Florida, ix, 67, 106, 119

Plan of Merger, 147-150, 158, 161

Prestwood, Charles, ix, 9-10, 14, 17, 33, 53-55, 60, 74, 101, 117, 118, 127, 129, 143

Purcell, Bishop Clare, 13, 30, 56, 60

Roberts, Henry, 157

Sanders, Bishop Carl J., 150-152